The Fraudulent Gospel

Politics and the World Council of Churches

BERNARD SMITH

Covenant Books
London

1991

ISBN 0-85205-020-8

First Edition published 1977

Second enlarged edition 1979

Third enlarged edition 1991

All editions copyright ©Bernard Smith

The earlier editions have been published in
Dutch, Swedish and Danish translations.

This book is dedicated
to my wife, Avril,
who journeyed with me

The Covenant Publishing Co. Ltd.
8 Blades Court, Deodar Road,
Putney, London, SW15 2NU.

Printed and bound in the United Kingdom by
Staples Printers Rochester Limited,
Love Lane, Rochester, Kent.

Table of Contents

    Acronyms... i

    About This Book... ii

    Introduction to Second Edition 1

1. WCC and African Terrorists 5
2. Education for Liberation 25
3. WCC and Black Power in Britain 33
4. WCC, Soviet Union and Human Rights 53
5. Georgi Vins and the WCC 73
6. Soviet Jews and the WCC 83
7. North American Indians and the WCC... 89
8. WCC and the Vietnam War 95
9. South Korea: Another Vietnam? 111
10. Missions and Marxism 121
11. WCC and the Theology of Anti-Christ... 127
12. Zimbabwe: a Failed Utopia 137
13. SWAPO: End of a Myth 143
14. Violence and the Churches in South Africa... ... 155

    Index 167

Acronyms

The abbreviations most commonly used in the book.

AIM	American Indian Movement.
ANC	African National Congress.
BCC	British Council of Churches: its name has recently been changed to The Council of Churches for Britain & Ireland.
CRRU	Community and Race Relations Unit of the BCC.
CWME	Commission on World Mission and Evangelism of the WCC.
ISHR	International Society for Human Rights.
NCC	Namibia Council of Churches.
PCR	Program to Combat Racism.
SACC	South African Council of Churches.
SADF	South African Defence Force.
SWAPO	South-West African People's Organization.
TRJ	Towards Racial Justice.
UDF	United Democratic Front.
UN	United Nations.
UNHCR	United Nations High Commissioner for Refugees.
WCC	World Council of Churches.

About This Book

THIS book *attacks* the World Council of Churches: it attacks with the weapons of reason and facts. When it was first published in 1977 it outraged many Christians but delighted many others and was widely read. In 1979 a second edition appeared to which some new material was added. After a few years the book went out of print and friends began urging me to prepare a third edition. I have left the main text unaltered but have added two chapters on African countries where WCC-backed terrorists have recently come to power: Robert Mugabe's Zimbabwe and SWAPO in Namibia. Both provide instructive lessons in the folly of trying to cast out Beelzebub by Beelzebub. A chapter on South Africa has also been added.

In the past year communist governments have been overthrown in Eastern Europe and even in Soviet Russia the communists' monopoly of power is challenged. The torrent of international events washes away the memory and we adjust to a new world forgetful of the old. But it is dangerous to have too short a memory: Solzhenitsyn quotes a Russian proverb, "He who forgets his own history is condemned to repeat it". This book records facts about the WCC that it would prefer us to forget: its careful silence about the evils of communism and its indifference to appeals for help from persecuted Christians: its financing of terrorists and its infatuation with Marxist revolution as a cure for the Third World's ills: its persistent denigration of America and the western democracies: its promotion of a sophisticated brand of ecumenism which regards the Christian gospel as an *obstacle* to the unification of mankind.

The WCC dispenses a generalised goodwill which many Christians find irresistible: it is thoroughly deceptive. If this book stimulates a more *critical* attitude towards the WCC it will have served a useful purpose.

Bernard Smith
Sussex, 1990

Introduction

THE World Council of Churches was founded in 1948. Its purpose was to further the aims of the "ecumenical movement" which had been growing rapidly in Europe for several decades. The ecumenical movement was basically an attempt to heal the divisions between different churches, but its agenda had never been limited to purely theological issues. It was also much concerned with working out a Christian social philosophy.

Questions such as war and peace, economic justice and internationalism were as likely to be discussed as rival doctrines of the eucharist. This social philosophy developed during the 1920s and 1930s and inevitably it owed more to the then currently fashionable Socialism than it did to Christianity. This was the tradition inherited by the newly-founded WCC.

At its first General Assembly held in 1948, delegates from 147 Protestant, Anglican and Orthodox Churches attended. By the 1975 Nairobi Assembly, the number of member churches had grown to 271. Almost all the major world churches are now members of the WCC; the chief exception is the Roman Catholic Church which, while still declining formal membership, works very closely with the WCC. 10% of the WCC's Commission on Faith and Order is made up of Roman Catholic theologians and the Vatican's Pontifical Commission for Justice and Peace and the WCC jointly run a committee on Society, Development and Peace (SODEPAX) which employs a common secretariat. In 1975, Pope Paul VI sent a personal gift of £4,000 to the WCC to help finance this committee. There is such close agreement between the Catholic Church and the WCC that Cardinal Jan Willebrands can write: ". . . the great problems and tasks that now confront the Churches are seen by the WCC and the Catholic Church in the same way, indeed they are also formulated in the same way."[1]

The WCC's offices in Geneva are now the headquarters of a complex world-wide organisation financed by annual grants from member churches. Every year the WCC disposes of vast amounts of money in aid of various kinds, mostly to Third World countries. Every seven years, it holds a general assembly to which delegates from member churches are invited. The founding assembly at Amsterdam in 1948 was followed by Evanston in 1954, New Delhi in 1961, Uppsala in 1968 and Nairobi in 1975. The value of such assemblies must largely depend on the quality of the delegates. What kind of people are they? An Anglican Bishop who attended reported that among the delegates "were very few representatives of what one might call the grass roots workers, local Church clergymen or lay readers from local groups. The trouble is that these kind of people have not usually time to spend in going to conferences, and unfortunately 'conference going' has become a kind of profession for some people. Most of these people are either members of the many different committees of the WCC or are paid workers of the Council. In between the big conferences they spend their time in writing and reading excellent articles and discussing them with one another, and then when the time comes, they go to the related conference stuffed with a great deal of intellectual data and exciting generalisations, but often not related to the many and varied local situations in small towns and villages throughout the world."[2]

However, real power lies not with the assemblies but with the Central Committee. This is the policy-making body that conducts the WCC's business in between assemblies. It is made up of 130 members representing member churches: the Church of England is represented

---

1. Cardinal Willebrands in an article 'Jesus Christ is Lord' in **L'Osservatore Romano,** 31 January, 1974.
2. The Anglican Bishop in Iran, The Rt. Revd. H. B. Dehquani-Tafti, discussing the WCC's Bangkok Conference in the journal **Theology,** February, 1974.

by the Bishop of Oxford and a laywoman. Since it is so powerful, the composition of the Central Committee is specially interesting. In 1973, the Bishop of Bristol, who was then a member of the Committee, gave this analysis of its membership:

Western White i.e. British, North American, Australian etc. 42%

Eastern Orthodox, mainly Russian, 28%

Non-White, mostly African but also Latin American and Third World, 30%.

The Bishop points out that a coalition of Russian Orthodox and Third Worlders gives a majority of 58% over white Westerners, and that 58% regards Westerners "primarily as the representatives of 'colonialism' with all the emotional overtones which that contains"[3] The Committee's political slant is suggested by the fact that at the time the Bishop made his analysis, it was reported that no more than a third of the Committee's members could be persuaded to sign a telegram to Mr. Brezhnev appealing to him to allow Solzhenitsyn to live with his family in Moscow.

In the 30 years of its existence, the WCC has become the most powerful opinion-making body in Christendom. This is partly because the member churches have too readily surrendered their authority and independence to the WCC. Church newspapers give generous space to WCC press releases, usually without any critical comment. Over the years the voice of the WCC has become louder while the churches have lapsed into quiescence. But a far more important factor than the weakness of the member churches has been the support which national Councils of Churches have given to the WCC. These Councils claim to be independent of the WCC, but, in fact, they act as agents of the WCC at the national level. "The fundamental aims of the British Council of Churches are very similar to the World Council" says the Revd. Harry Morton,

---

3. Bishop of Bristol in a letter in the **Church Times**, 7 September 1973.

general secretary of the BCC. The BCC has always dutifully rubber-stamped the WCC's policies on all important political issues. Chapter three of the present book shows how the BCC and the WCC collaborated to support a militant Black Power group in London. The BCC is at present urging British Churches to make donations to the highly controversial WCC Special Fund which dispenses grants to African terrorists and has opened a special bank account to receive these contributions. In all other Western countries, the national Councils of Churches have played the same supportive role to "Big Brother". This is especially true of the USA where the former president of the National Council of Churches, Dr. Eugene Carson Blake, later became secretary general of the WCC. In Rhodesia, the national Council is actually required by the WCC's Constitution to carry out WCC policies.

The WCC likes to describe itself as "an instrument at the service of the churches" and its Constitution expressly disclaims any right to speak for member churches. That is surely hypocritical. Bishop Kenneth Sansbury, when he was leader of the BCC, was more frank. He spoke of the "thoughtless and reactionary in the pew" and said that the BCC must always be "a little ahead of the main body of churchgoers".[4] The WCC is equally impatient with the conservative majority of mankind and nowhere is this more evident than in its infatuation with revolutionary politics. "In recent years the WCC has displayed a political bias recognisably Marxist in its preference for social revolution of a Leftward character over any spiritual initiative of Christian mission in the world".[5] When that can be said in the editorial column of Britain's leading Anglican newspaper, it is surely time for Christians to look more critically at this body.

This study is, I hope, a contribution towards that end.

Bernard Smith
London, July 1977

---

4. Bishop Sansbury reported in **Church Times**, 24 April 1970.
5. **Church Times** editorial 21 November 1975.

Chapter I

WCC AND AFRICAN TERRORISTS

NO other action of the World Council of Churches has aroused such bitter controversy as its grants to African terrorists. Starting in 1970, it has now given over £500,000 to groups actually engaged in guerilla warfare. The WCC has frankly admitted that the grants are intended to demonstrate its moral support for the justice of the terrorists' cause and their political objectives.

It was a difficult pill for some in the churches to swallow, but it was given a coating of sugary assurances that the grants were intended solely for "humanitarian purposes" — social, health, educational and legal aid purposes. At the same time, the WCC declared that the "grants are made without control of the manner in which they are spent". How, then, could the WCC be sure that money given to terrorists for "humanitarian" purposes was not spent on arms? In the year that the first grants were made, Dr. Blake, who at the time was general secretary of the WCC, candidly admitted that there could be no guarantee "that funds destined for liberation movements might not be used to buy weapons". In 1975, his successor, Dr. Philip Potter, questioned on the same issue, stated that the WCC "would not send inspectors to see whether the money had been spent in the way that it was given — and for a good reason. There could be no real sense of solidarity with people if you did not trust them."[1] These admissions should be more widely known: they mean that those who contribute money to the WCC for these grants take precisely the same chance of their money being used to buy guns as those Irish Americans who respond

---
1. Dr. Potter speaking in Glasgow, May 1975.

to the appeals of IRA support groups such as "Northern Aid" in the USA. They also are told that their donations will be used exclusively for "humanitarian" purposes.

The grants made many people who had not previously been critical of the WCC experience their first doubts. The WCC, representing some 250 member churches, was seen to be supporting openly terrorist groups whose methods of gaining their ends were every bit as inhuman as those of the IRA; whose ideologies were Marxist and many of whose leaders had been trained in the arts of guerilla warfare in Soviet Russia; whose arms were obtained from the Soviet Union, Eastern Europe, China and North Korea and whose goal was the violent overthrow of the governments of Rhodesia, South Africa, South-West Africa, Mozambique, Angola and Guinea-Bissau.

Commenting on the first grants in September 1970, the **Times** newspaper observed: "On the face of it, Christian authorities have no business to support organisations which are engaged in the use of terror, whatever their grievances and however sincere they may be".[2] In the controversy that followed those first grants that point has often been obscured. Yet it is, for the Christian, the heart of the matter. If the essence of terrorism is the unprovoked attack on the innocent civilian, then the **Times** is surely right. There are occasions when the Christian is justified in using violence, but never in using terrorism.

The WCC has never admitted that the word "terrorist" can be rightly applied to the groups it supports: it refers to them as "liberation movements". The refusal of the WCC and its apologists to face the facts about the groups it supports renders its whole discussion of the moral issues unreal and irrelevant. WCC committees and working parties discuss abstract "violence" at great length and produce wordy reports on the subject. But their deliberations are valueless since they will not accept that it is not violence in general which constitutes the moral issue but terrorism in particular. Indeed, any attempt to intro-

---

2. **Times,** 15 September 1970.

duce the concept of terrorism into the discussion is usually dismissed as "emotive".

The present writer debated this issue on BCC Radio 4 with the Revd. Elliott Kendall of he British Council of Churches and the following is an extract from the transcript :

Interviewer: Mr. Smith is very concerned that what you describe as freedom fighters are in fact plain terrorists.

Kendall: Well, terrorists are people who use terror for its own purposes or for the sake of terror. I think those of us who are closely in touch with the liberation movements in Africa know that these groups are really struggling for political independence and the use of the description "terrorist" is not acceptable and it isn't really an adequate description.

Interviewer: Their methods have been pretty violent though; are they justified?

Kendall: Their methods are the methods of armed struggle. I think one would say that on the whole the liberation movements in Africa have been acting responsibly in their armed struggle and the use of terrorism is not really a correct description.[3]

Let us see just how "responsibly" these "liberation movements" have been acting. Consider the following newspaper reports :

Guerillas beat school head to death

"Five guerillas entered the Mangare school in the Kandeya tribal trust in NE Rhodesia on Saturday night and dragged the headmaster, Mr. Chipara, from his home. After forcing him to hand over books and money, they lined up three teachers, one of them the headmaster's brother, and beat Mr. Chipara to death". **(Daily Telegraph,** 29 August, 1973).

Terrorist forced man to eat own ears

"Another case of brutality by guerillas operating in Rhodesia's north-eastern border area has been reported.

---

3. BBC Radio 4 "Sunday" programme, 3 July, 1975.

A tribesman, Mr. Phillip Humane, aged 30, had his ears cut off and was forced to eat them. Then most of his toes and fingers were hacked off . . . Mr. Humane said a gang of about 17 guerillas had also gone to his father-in-law's house and beaten him to death. The gang came to his village early on Monday night and accused him of visiting a security force camp . . . One member of the gang then took a bayonet from his rifle and hacked off Mr. Humane's ears. After trying to cut off his nose the gang made him eat his ears. The guerillas then made his wife fetch an axe and the man who had hacked off his ears then used the axe to hack off Mr. Humane's fingers and toes. He had not lost consciousness during the attack and when he asked for mercy they told him they wanted him to suffer. This is the second case of enforced cannibalism in the border area. Last December a tribesman had his nose, ears, lips and chin hacked off and his wife was forced to eat them." (**Times,** 19 February, 1976).

These are two of many similar incidents that have been reported. Unhappily they cannot be dismissed as the excesses of a few undisciplined and isolated groups of terrorists. There is a great deal of evidence to show that these acts are part of a **deliberate policy** of terrorising the African people. Its object is to frighten them into supporting the terrorists. A BBC observer in Mozambique reporting in 1974 said that "Frelimo is gradually giving up any attempt at winning over the African population and is instead resorting to undiluted terrorism to cow the population into co-operation with raiding groups".[4] This policy of terrorising **their own people** accounts for the fact that the vast majority of those killed and injured in their campaigns are **Africans** and not Europeans. In 1974, for example, terrorist attacks in Rhodesia resulted in the murder of 150 African civilians and only five Europeans.

Striking evidence of the terrorising of ordinary African workers by the "liberation" movement ZANU, to which the WCC has given large sums of money, was given in a

---

4. John Osman, BBC Radio 4, 1 February 1974.

court in Salisbury, Rhodesia, in March 1975. The court had met to consider the continuing detention of the Revd. Sithole, president of ZANU. During the hearing the president of the court read out the details of the murder by ZANU terrorists of 32 African civilians, all of which were committed in a brief period of about three months. The following are typical examples:

Kandeya Tribal Trust Land: On 17 December, 1974 three terrorists arrived at a kraal 11 km ENE of Mount Darwin and sought out a villager whom they accused of working for the CID. He denied these allegations and offered the terrorists money, but he was bound and beaten to death with sticks and an axe.

Ngarwe TTL: On the evening of 17 February, 1975 eight terrorists visited a kraal 25 km south of Nyamapanda, summoned the kraalhead and beat him. His wife was ordered from the kraal, and while leaving heard a burst of automatic fire which killed her husband.

Chikwise TTL: at 22.30 hours on 19 March 1975, three terrorists visited a kraal 27 km SSW of Nyamapanda, sought out two tribesmen, stood them up against their hut and threw a stick grenade at them. One was killed instantly, and as the second tried to crawl away he was shot and killed.[6]

More recently in December 1976 there has been the butchering of 27 African labourers which the **Times** newspaper described as "the most cold-blooded massacre yet seen in Rhodesia's bush war". The Revd. Arthur Lewis, an Anglican mission priest, visited the scene. "I have just paid a flying visit to my old mission district of St. Peter's Mission on the eastern border of Rhodesia. Terrorists from Mozambique had force-marched the occupants of a whole workers' village at night to the lighted factory of a nearby tea-estate. The women and children were placed apart from the menfolk, who were compelled to lie down and were then shot in cold blood before their families. Automatic weapons of Communist manufacture were used. The

---

5. **Judgement.** Rhodesian Ministry of Information, April 1975.

corpses we saw were a ghastly and pathetic sight, having in some cases been bayoneted after being shot: the families with whom I spoke and prayed were utterly distraught. Twenty-seven men were killed, eleven were injured and two escaped by jumping into a river en route. The terrorists addressed each other as 'Comrade' . . . "

Fr. Lewis adds the comment: "Since the terrorist organisations are actively encouraged, through the so-called Programme to Combat Racism, by the WCC and other religious bodies, the Marxist infiltration of Christian Churches and organisations is now demonstrated beyond possible dispute".

If we are to follow the WCC in calling these butchers "liberators" rather than terrorists, we must surely ask who are they liberating? Not the innocent people they terrorise. When is a terrorist not a terrorist? That is a pertinent question. Solzhenitsyn has said: "When we are attacked, it's terrorism, but when we do the attacking, it's a guerilla movement of liberation".

In January 1973, the Anglican Bishops of Mashonaland and Matabeleland in Rhodesia wrote to the WCC protesting that the WCC was financing groups that "employ methods of naked terrorism". They said the terrorists "came out of the bush, surrounded farmhouses by night, sprayed them with bullets and heavier armaments, wounding occupants, chiefly children, and burning down houses of local Africans".

The WCC ignored their protest.

In May 1974, they wrote again. Since their last letter, they said, "members of ZANU and their willing or forced accomplices have killed 87 civilians in this country. Far and away the majority of these have been Africans, innocent of any offence and most have been killed with great brutality. Others have been abducted, raped, beaten and disfigured". The Bishops ended their letter: "We have learnt with disgust that earlier this year £6,355 was voted (by the WCC) to ZANU".

Later that same year the Bishop of Mashonaland, writing in the journal **Theology**, said: "I write in a diocese which has experienced hundreds of guerilla fighters entering it from Frelimo bases to meet death themselves, but also to mete out dreadful deaths and torture to Africans in far greater numbers than to the few Europeans who have been murdered". He goes on to speak of atrocities by Frelimo, a group which at that time had received over £50,000 from the WCC. "These atrocities were not merely attested by the Portuguese but by the former Frelimo fighters and Maconde tribesmen who witnessed them at the "julgamento publico" sessions which went on year after year. One former Frelimo leader, Mr. Uria Simango, claimed in his book **Situacao sombria na Frelimo,** that these massacres numbered thousands."[6]

The WCC insists on regarding "liberation" movements as "instruments of peace, human dignity, equality and justice". It is not surprising, therefore, that it has never rebuked them for their atrocities. Nor is it surprising that it makes grants to terrorists without requiring, as a condition of acceptance, that all terrorist practices should cease. As if to complicate the issue, the WCC has made a quite explicit condemnation of terrorism. The report in which it appears was the result of two years' study so it may be assumed to express the WCC's considered judgement:

"There are some forms of violence in which Christians may not participate and which the churches must condemn. There are violent causes — the conquest of one people by another or the deliberate oppression of one class or race by another — which offend divine justice. There are violent means of struggle — torture in all forms, the holding of innocent hostages and the deliberate or indiscriminate killing of innocent non-combatants for example — which destroy the soul of the perpetrator as surely as the life and health of the victim".[7] The WCC condemns terrorism and asserts that a Christian may have no part in it. At the same time, it gives its approval to the political goals of African terrorists; blandly ignores the brutality of

---

6. **Theology, July 1974.**
7. **Violence, Non-violence and the Struggle for Social Justice,** published by WCC, 1973.

their methods, and glosses over the contradiction by calling them "liberators".

The WCC is not alone in this: many prominent churchmen have been similarly split in two over their abhorrence of terrorist methods and their wish to see white governments in Africa overthrown. It is a struggle in which politics always defeats moral principle. Rt. Revd. Trevor Huddleston, Bishop of Stepney, who is a pacifist, resolves the problem by calling terrorists patriots. "While I could never visit a guerilla army training camp and give them my blessing, you will never get me to describe the people engaged in guerilla activity as evil men or terrorists. They are patriots. I would consider them exactly on a level with the French underground forces at work during the Nazi occupation."[8] It is a little surprising to find a pacifist arguing that patriotism excuses otherwise inexcusable acts. Another Anglican pacifist, the Revd. Paul Oestreicher, is prevented by his scruples from actually using a machine-gun but nevertheless feels free to buy them for those who will. "Meanwhile if, in their freedom as God's children (but not necessarily as Christians), the oppressed and their friends see no better way of bringing the day of freedom nearer than by buying machine-guns, that is their right. We should be where the action (and suffering) is, with them . . . at least in our allegiance and with our cheque book".[9]

More honest than either of these is the Methodist minister Revd. Colin Morris. He spent many years in Zambia and became a close friend of President Kenneth Kaunda. He has no illusions about terrorists and wastes no time in inventing euphemisms for them. "Force in Rhodesia", he writes, "can only mean a messy guerila warfare which in order to be effective must include a high degree of terrorism — throwing petrol bombs through farmhouse windows, the ambushing of civilian cars, night-strikes against isolated homesteads. . . "[10]

---

8. **Church Times** report, 18 July 1969.
9. Article in Anglican Pacifist Fellowship's **Challenge**, February 1970.
10. **Unyoung, Uncoloured, Unpoor** by Colin Morris, London 1969, p. 28.

A Christian minister might be expected, after such a realistic assessment of terrorism, to assert unequivocally that it is contrary to the Gospel and that no Christian should support, condone or approve it. But no. In the same book from which I have quoted the above, Dr. Morris says: "I believe freedom fighters are justified in using any methods short of sadistic cruelty for its own sake to overthrow the Salisbury regime."[11] Since Dr. Morris wrote that book, he has become general secretary of the Methodist Missionary Society which has donated about £8,000 to the WCC's Special Fund from which grants to guerilla are drawn. (Only two other church bodies in this country have made gifts to the Fund — the Iona Community and the Congregational Union of Scotland). Presumably none of the atrocities detailed earlier in this chapter would be considered by Dr. Morris to be "sadistic cruelty for its own sake": but it is surely a strange use for mission society funds. After a television programme in which Dr. Morris was questioned by the present writer on the morality of MMS grants to terrorists, the **Methodist Recorder's** TV critic remarked: "The MMS emerged from the remarks of Dr. Morris as a body concerned about people in Christian Love . . ." Capping that is the comment by Mr. Allan Shaw, Methodist lay delegate to the WCC's Nairobi Assembly in 1975: "Those who are fighting for liberation do so in love and not in hate". Such remarks are hardly worth refuting; they suggest that sanctimonious humbug was not a vice peculiar to the Victorians.

Since the early 1960s, there has been a gradually mounting wave of terrorism throughout the civilised world. The terrorist has become the scourge of ordered society. Putting his bomb in a brief case, the terrorist can enter the city centre, leave his bomb at a cinema, restaurant, or in a train and leave again as unnoticed as he came. A small army of dedicated and ruthless terrorists can — as in Northern Ireland — keep a whole police force and army at bay; keep civilians in a state of perpetual anxiety and cause immense damage to property and persons. What

---

11. Ibid. p. 1.

should be the attitude of governments, political parties and churches to this threat to ordered society? Undoubtedly it should be a determination to wage ceaseless war against the enemy until terrorism is eradicated. Until this is done, governments have not discharged their first duty to ordinary people, which is to secure the conditions of civilised life from the threat of violent disruption. When there is a failure of will by the government, as in the Lebanon, anarchy prevails.

Western governments have been lamentably weak in dealing with terrorists. In November 1974, it was necessary for Lord Chalfont to begin an article in the **Times** with this sentence: "It is high time that the civilised world declared open war on political terrorism".[12] The reasons for the weakness of government are many and they cannot be explored here. But this much is certain: their resolve to combat the terrorist would have been greatly strengthened if the **Churches** had clearly and unambiguously condemned terrorism. Church leaders have failed to do so, although there have been many occasions when they might have spoken plainly.

The fact is that the Churches are in no position to utter such denunciations of terrorism since their authority on this issue has been fatally compromised. How can they exhort governments to stand firm against the terrorist when through their membership of the WCC, they themselves are implicated in the encouragement of terrorism? When Dr. Coggan, Archbishop of Canterbury, went to Dublin in May 1975 and called for an end to financial support for para-military groups in Northern Ireland, he should also have gone to Geneva and appealed to the WCC to stop giving money to para-military groups in Africa. An act of terrorism is no less wicked in Africa than it is in Northern Ireland. If the Church wishes to condemn one, it must also condemn the other. The failure of the Churches in the West — and I include the Roman Catholic Church — to give government and people a clear directive in this matter must involve them in a grave loss of moral status.

---

12 **Times,** 25 November 1974.

That this should happen at a time when the West is enfeebled by neurotic self-questionings and doubts is proof of how unreliable the Churches are in the present crisis.

Terrorism and the WCC: the storm breaks

Since writing the first edition, the long catalogue of terrorist atrocities in Rhodesia culminated in June 1978 with the slaughter of eight British Pentecostal missionaries and their four children. (A ninth missionary died later from wounds, thus bringing the total of missionaries killed by Rhodesian terrorists to 37.) The terrorists surprised the missionaries, at their lonely Elim mission school, in the middle of the night. Together with their children, a girl of five, a boy of six and a three-week-old baby, the missionaries were taken from their beds and led through a wood to the edge of a cricket pitch. The six women were first raped and then butchered with exceptional savagery. The faces of every adult were mutilated and the eyes of one man were gouged out after bayonetting him in the back 15 times. The doctor who conducted the post mortem said there had been an attempt to rape the four-year-old girl. She had then been kicked so hard in the face with a heavy boot that it left an imprint, bayonetted in the arms and legs and finally killed by crushing her skull.[13] Hardened newspaper correspondents who were allowed to see the bodies were shocked by the savagery.

In Britain, memorial services for the victims were held in Elim churches throughout the country. The Foreign Secretary, Dr. David Owen, described the killings as "senseless and shocking". A public statement by the Archbishop of Canterbury recording the nation's feelings was no doubt expected by many: it did not come. None of the British church leaders made any public denunciation of the killers. But did they need to? Had not Robert Mugabe, one of the leaders of the Patriotic Front, denied

---

13. Letter from Dr. Anthony David Owen in the South African Christian newspaper **Encounter,** September 1978.

that the massacre was the work of his terrorists? He blamed it onto the Rhodesian security forces. Bishop Lamont, deported from Rhodesia for aiding terrorists, once called Mugabe a "dedicated Catholic". Of course, no one believed Mr. Mugabe; no one, that is, outside the churches. The WCC had been trying for a long time to convince church people that atrocities said to be committed by the terrorists were in fact the work of the Selous Scouts, the Rhodesian army's crack anti-terrorist squad. According to this theory the Scouts blacked their faces, carried Communist rifles and spoke in African dialects to commit atrocities which would then be laid at the door of the Patriotic Front. Many in the churches were gullible enough to believe that this was so. Church leaders could be sure of a docile hearing when they spoke from their pulpits but public statements were a very different matter. They could hardly condemn the Patriotic Front since through the WCC grants they were supporting it against Ian Smith's government. Yet with public feeling still inflamed by accounts of the massacre it was far too risky to suggest that the terrorists were not to blame. In this dilemma the church leaders decided, as often before, on a prudent silence.

When the Rev Paul Oestreicher, a spokesman for the British Council of Churches and chairman of the British section of Amnesty, was asked if he thought the WCC would now stop grants to Rhodesian terrorists, his discomfort was apparent; "I certainly don't think they will withdraw their aid. They have supplied all sorts of groups for humanitarian purposes. There have been dreadful atrocities committed by both sides. The actions of the murderers have been totally condemned by Mr. Mugabe. The massacre was damnable, whoever did it — but we don't absolutely know who did it."[14] Not many days after Mr. Oestreicher said that, Rhodesian soldiers, following tracks from the scene of the massacre, shot two Patriotic Front terrorists. On one was found a tape of the Elim boy's choir,

---

14. **Church Times**, 30 June 1978.

stolen on the night of the massacre, and a diary describing how he and 20 others had murdered their victims with axes and knobkerries.

On 11 August 1978, less than three weeks after the massacre, came the news of a grant of nearly £45,000 from the WCC to the Patriotic Front. The two-inch capitals on the front page of the **Daily Express** were fully justified: "BLOOD MONEY — Rhodesian mission killers get cash aid — courtesy of world's churches". The WCC could not be wholly insensitive to the public's feelings. It must have known that there would be a violent reaction and that many would see the grant as a reward to the murderers of the missionaries. What could the WCC hope to gain from this seemingly deliberate affront to public sensibilities? Very little. But perhaps the WCC could afford the risk of further alienating the general public if it could strengthen its support in the churches. Viewed like this the grant may have been a calculated test of the depth of the churches' political commitment. Would the member churches flinch from giving aid to those who had so recently slaughtered missionaries? Or would they stifle their moral misgivings and push on, unencumbered, towards the political goal? Some might defect but the majority would surely remain loyal. The WCC would emerge from the crisis strengthened. She would know who were her most reliable allies and who could be counted on in the future. Rhodesia, after all, was only a preliminary skirmish: South Africa was to come.

Whatever the WCC's reasons may have been, the immediate effect of the grant was a storm of protest. Leaders of many denominations reported a surge of angry letters and phone calls from church members. Typical of many parish churches was the petition signed by more than 100 parishioners in the village of Brede, near Rye in Sussex. It called on the British Council of Churches to discourage the sending of more funds from Britain to support the Patriotic Front which, it said, "is openly seeking to establish a Marxist regime in Rhodesia by murder and terror". The rector of Brede claimed that the petition voiced the opinion of 98% of those who attended his church.[15]

Quickly the Church leaders moved to suppress the movement of dissent. The Lambeth Conference was in session when the grant was announced and the following day, there was an attempt by a handful of bishops to persuade the Conference to denounce the WCC and its grant. Bishop Paul Burrough of Mashonaland offered to give his fellow bishops "terrible details" of what the Patriotic Front had done in his own diocese. But the bishops were not interested. The Bishop of Manchester, a former WCC official, proposed a motion urging Anglicans to "reaffirm their support and strengthen their understanding" of the WCC. There was an overwhelming vote in favour.

And so 450 Anglican bishops at Lambeth judiciously avoided the moral problem posed by the Church's support for terrorism. But others did not find evasion so easy. On 21 August, the Salvation Army announced that it had been "perplexed and distressed" by the WCC grant and was therefore suspending its membership "pending inquiries". The Army was not getting involved in politics, explained Colonel Wesley Harris: "It is the use of violence to which we raise our objections".[16] In acting as it did, the Salvation Army undoubtedly earned the gratitude of many Christians in other churches. The Army had done what they wanted their own church leaders to do. They knew that terrorism was wrong and they knew that the WCC was wrong to sanction terrorism. They also suspected that their own church leaders would find some very sophisticated arguments to prove them mistaken. The Army had set a shining example; it had had the courage to dissent. "Suspension" was not the same as complete withdrawal from the WCC but it nevertheless implied a healthy determination to criticise WCC policy. If more churches followed it might be possible to curb the worst of the WCC's excesses. But would more follow?

At the beginning of September, the fires of public hostility towards the Patriotic Front and the WCC were re-

---

15. **Sunday Telegraph,** 20 August 1978.
16. **Guardian,** 22 August 1978.

fuelled by the news that the terrorists had shot down a Rhodesian Viscount civilian aircraft killing 34 passengers in the crash. Of the 18 who survived, 10 were lined up by the terrorists and deliberately bayonetted and shot to death. The act was witnessed by the remaining eight survivors who had escaped unseen into the surrounding undergrowth. The WCC, which had made no comment on the massacre of the missionaries, now issued a press release. It was obliged to do so since Joshua Nkomo, one of the leaders of the Patriotic Front, had openly admitted shooting down the plane although he denied the massacre of the survivors. The text of the press release read:

"A spokesman of the WCC said today that the Council 'deeply deplores the reported shooting down of a civilian aircraft in Rhodesia'. He added that at the same time as deploring this action the Council strongly condemns the killings of thousands of defenceless African civilians in refugee camps inside Rhodesia and in neighbouring countries. 'This latest action only reinforces the WCC's earlier stated position which supports efforts to achieve a just and peaceful settlement through negotiations involving all the parties concerned and in the interests of them all'. said the spokesman."

It is noticeable that there is no mention of the Patriotic Front although the Front had admitted its guilt in the matter. The statement "deplores" the incident of the shooting down of the plane but "strongly condemns" alleged atrocities of the Rhodesian security forces. The final sentence seems to attach guilt for the shooting down of the plane to those who obstruct "negotiations involving all the parties concerned" rather than to the Front. Such tortuous dishonesty is characteristic of WCC statements. It is instructive to compare the WCC's statement with a sermon delivered by John da Costa, Dean of Salisbury (Rhodesia) at a memorial service in Salisbury Cathedral for those who died. Here is a part of the sermon:

"Nobody who holds sacred the dignity of human life can be anything but sickened at the events attending the crash of the Viscount. Survivors have the greatest call on the sympathy and assistance of every other human being. The horror of the crash was bad enough, but that this should have been compounded by murder of the most savage and treacherous sort, leaves us stunned with disbelief and brings revulsion in the minds of anyone deserving the name 'human'. This bestiality, worse than anything in recent history, stinks in the nostrils of heaven.

"But are we deafened with the voice of protest from nations which call themselves 'civilised'? We are not! Like men in the story of the Good Samaritan they pass by on the other side. One listens for the loud condemnation by Dr. David Owen, himself a medical doctor, trained to extend mercy and help to all in need. One listens and the silence is deafening. One listens for loud condemnations by the President of the United States, himself a man from the Bible-Baptist belt, and again the silence is deafening. One listens for loud condemnation by the Pope, by the Chief Rabbi, by the Archbishop of Canterbury, by all who love the name of God. Again the silence is deafening."

Throughout August, September and October, letters for and against the WCC's grant fizzed and banged like firecrackers in the pages of church newspapers. There were angry calls for withholding money from church collections, a suggestion supported in the leading article of at least two national newspapers. An article by Mr. Ronald Butt appeared in the **Times** on 14 September. He wrote: "Speaking for myself, I think the time has come for the application of sanctions against the WCC and the BCC. Since the leaders of the church prefer silence (why have the archbishops and bishops not condemned without compromise the recent actions of Mr. Nkomo?) perhaps the laity could speak for them . . . If we wish to stop the bureaucracy of politically minded WCC clerics from their present conduct, the churches will have to stop the money that supports their organisation. But how can we persuade the supine church leaders in Britain to do this? . . . If all churchgoers would decline to put any money in the church boxes for a week or two, replacing it with a note saying why, I think that the minds and the consciences of the leaders of the Church would be greatly concentrated . . ."

Parish churches had, in fact, a very effective means of applying financial sanctions to the Church: they could refuse to pass on any of their income to the diocese. There were enough reports of parishes doing this to compel the general secretary of the Anglican General Synod to deprecate it in the course of a long letter to the church press.[17] His defence of the Church's failure to condemn the WCC's grant was a familiar exercise in church diplomacy and can have influenced no one.

Late in October, the BCC met in London. With Dr. Coggan presiding, the Council declared that "no new issue of principle" had been raised by the WCC's grant to the Patriotic Front, and, therefore, there was no reason why it should not be approved. It was certainly a fact that the recent grant was no different in principle from any of the previous grants. The WCC, without any complaint from member churches, had been making such grants to terrorists since 1970. Why should the churches now be expected to protest? Merely to gratify public indignation? Had not missionaries been killed before? The total of dead missionaries was now 37: the time for raising objections of principle was long since past.

No one familiar with the BCC's attitude towards Rhodesia would have expected it to behave any differently. Since 1965, when Rhodesia declared her independence, the BCC had been inflexibly hostile towards Ian Smith's government. On the occasion of UDI, the BCC was prepared to fight a holy war: "As Christians we have to say that it will be right to use force" said the Archbishop of Canterbury, Dr. Michael Ramsey. The next day he sent a private message to Prime Minister Mr. Harold Wilson: "The British Council of Churches ardently supports you . . . if you and your government should judge it necessary to use force to sustain our country's obligations, I am sure a great body of Christian opinion would support you". Plainly embarrassed by the Archbishop's zeal for war, Mr.

---

17. **Church Times,** 1 September 1978.

Wilson referred to Dr. Ramsey's message a few days later in the House of Commons: "The government do not believe that this is a constitutional problem that can be settled by the use of force", he said.

On the very same day that the Archbishop sent his private message to Mr. Wilson, the Anglican Bishop of Mashonaland in Rhodesia, wrote to the national papers in Britain warning that the use of force would cause "undying hatred between Britain and thousands of her sons and daughters and would have appalling consequences for Rhodesia and for the whole of Southern Africa".

The BCC had failed to enlist the support of Mr. Harold Wilson and his administration in its bid to overthrow Ian Smith by force of arms. 13 years later, it is unlikely to repudiate those who are fighting Mr. Smith even if their methods — slaughtering missionaries — are rather unChristian. In those intervening years the BCC has done everything in its power to give moral support to the terrorists. In 1976, it went as far as it dared in giving financial backing to the WCC's Programme to Combat Racism: it appointed itself a collecting agency for the Special Fund. It encouraged churches and private persons to contribute to the Fund and opened a special bank account to receive the donations. In 1977 it published a pamphlet entitled: **Rhodesia Now: the Liberation of Zimbabwe.** This described the terrorists as "Christian soldiers" and urged Christians in Britain to support them. It admitted that this step "may make the war more terrible" . . . but . . . "In the light of conscience, Christians in Britain should give the most effective support possible to the struggle for self-determination". What such a "struggle" really meant was better understood by the Anglican Bishop of Matabeleland, Anselm Genders, who wrote,

"You can imagine how encouraged we are by the thought that those who bayonet a six-month-old baby to death, or cut off a man's genitals and leave him to bleed to death in the sun, or cut off a man's lips and make his wife cook and eat them, are receiving moral and financial support from the British Council of Churches. A man is known by the company he keeps; so is the BCC".[18]

This same bishop, when he heard of the BCC's decision to approve the WCC's grant to the Patriotic Front, sent the following cable to the BCC:

"Judas Iscariot, Patron Saint of World Council. British support for World Council motivated by British love of blood sports". On the same day that he heard the news of the BCC's decision, one of his black priests had to flee from his rural parish because of the activities of Patriotic Front terrorists: he feared for his life and his family's.

Early in November, the Anglican Church's General Synod met at Church House, Westminster. After a six-and-a-half hour debate on women priests, there was just $1\frac{3}{4}$ hours left to debate the WCC's controversial grant. The Bishop of Bath and Wells proposed a motion which he candidly admitted was intended to defuse a dangerous situation. Mild as it was, it was not mild enough for the Synod. Canon Douglas Rhymes objected to the motion because it claimed that the WCC's grant had caused "outrage". He proposed that the word "controversy" be substituted and his amendment was duly carried. Another amendment, which was also accepted, recalled approvingly that the Lambeth Conference had urged the Church to reaffirm its support for and understanding of the WCC. The Bishop defended the grant theologically by saying, "we took a leaf out of the Magnificat . . . in which the Virgin Mary herself talks about putting down the mighty and exalting the meek." Attempts to give the motion some bite were promptly rejected by Synod. An amendment that sought to dissociate the Anglican Church from the grant was overwhelmingly defeated. Another, put in the last few minutes after extra time for debate had been refused, called for "an assurance from the WCC that no support be given to unlawful killing of innocent people of any race in any country by terrorists." Although the proposer of this amendment was left with only three minutes in which to explain it, she was twice interrupted on points of

---

18. *Christian World*, 4 May 1978.

order by the Revd. Paul Oestreicher, an official of the BCC. There was no need to vote on this amendment: the Synod's derisive treatment of it was conclusive enough.

So the Anglican General Synod followed the Lambeth Conference and the British Council of Churches in what was now clearly the "official line". It amounted to an eleventh commandment: thou shalt not criticise the WCC. Peace could be bought — but at what price? The anger and discontent of many church members was likely to be increased rather than assuaged by the evasion of full and frank debate. Their voice had not yet been given a fair hearing but they would not be silenced for ever.

In other churches, the position was very different. In West Germany the Lutheran-Evangelical Church of Schaumburg-Lippe, following the example of the Salvation Army, suspended its membership of the WCC. Towards the end of November, the Presbyterian Church in Ireland held a special meeting of over 1,000 delegates and ministers. After a five hour debate the assembly voted by 561 to 393 — a majority of 168 — to suspend membership of the WCC in protest against the grant to the Patriotic Front. Complete withdrawal may come in two years' time if the next general assembly votes in the same way.

Controversy will continue to erupt for a long time to come and other churches may secede from the WCC. But the leaders of all churches will do their utmost to discourage criticism and impede discussion. A recent example of this sort of obscurantism was provided in May 1978 when the trustees of the Methodist Central Hall in Westminster peremptorily cancelled a booking by an international group of anti-Marxist theologians. Explaining their reasons for doing so, the Revd. Dr. Barnett and the Revd. Kenneth Greet, both leading Methodists, said that since the Methodist Church was a member of the WCC the trustees could not countenance a meeting at which the WCC would be criticised. Later in the same year a meeting of prostitutes was held in Central Hall to promote a campaign for legalising prostitution. It is not recorded that either Dr. Barnett or Dr. Greet objected.

Chapter II

EDUCATION FOR LIBERATION

THE Charity Schools that pioneered mass education in this country believed in teaching children to read, write and learn good manners. It was taken for granted that the only book they were likely to read was the Bible.

Every year we spend more and more money on education and our children spend more and more time in schools. Yet we seem further than ever from any understanding of what it's all for.

There was a time — before the last war — when we thought that the purpose of education was to equip us to earn a living. Now we know that isn't so — at least, our philosophers of education have told us it isn't so. They disparage such practical and plebeian notions as earning a living. "Education", they say, "is for Life . . . for Leisure . . . to develop the Personality . . . to encourage a mature response to the challenge of the social environment" . . . and so on.

The World Council of Churches has not been left behind in this Gadarene rush to produce novel philosophies of education. There is, of course, every reason why a Christian body should occupy itself with education: education has always been a part of Christian mission both at home and overseas and for two centuries the mission school was a frontier outpost of expanding European civilisation. The WCC is proud to trace back its own interest in education to the Sunday School conventions of the nineteenth century. But Victorian worthies would surely be surprised to discover that the WCC's educational goals are now "the transformation of society" and the "liberation of the dispossessed".

In 1973, a WCC meeting was held at Geneva to discuss 'Education and Theology in the Context of the Struggle for

Liberation'. The report of that meeting gives a very clear picture of how education is to be used to revolutionize society.

" 'In the long run', said one group speaking for all, 'there is no use speaking of change in the field of education without change in the whole structure of society'. Further, it was noted that the oppressors — those who now gain from the status quo — cannot be expected to approve of liberating education. It must come from the common struggle of those who are oppressed . . . After analysing oppression and liberation, the participants studied together the **educational processes** by which they are attempting to work towards the liberation of people. Traditional schools were criticised as one of the major ways by which the dominating forces in society perpetuated their dominance, inculcating into younger generations an acceptance of the status quo . . . Some attacked 'excellence' as a Christian goal for education, saying that it allowed Christian institutions to serve the elite of society and thus maintain in power those who in fact are the oppressors . . . One educational method appeared again and again: **engagement in action as a way of learning** 'To know reality one must plunge into it and share it'. 'The fight is the best teacher'. Only when one is engaged with those in the struggle can he help them frame the questions that bring awareness of the forces that oppress them. Thus one seeks out the conflict elements in each situation, for it is in the awareness of conflict that a sense of class emerges".[1]

That is a frankly Marxist view of education: the ruling class uses education to keep the people in subjection, but when the people have been taught the facts about the class struggle, they will liberate themselves by violence and a just society will emerge. One of the aims of the early Communists, according to Marx and Engels in **The Communist Manifesto,** was "to rescue education from the influence of the ruling class".[2]

---

1. **This Month.** July 1975, pp 10-11. A WCC publication.
2. **The Communist Manifesto.** Marx & Engels. Pelican ed. 1974. p. 100.

In a WCC booklet expounding "education for liberation", a strip cartoon is used to show what it would mean for the peasants of the Third World. The first picture is of a ragged, straw-hatted peasant with a ball and chain on his leg. The caption reads: "This is an uneducated Third World Man". In the second picture there is the same peasant and the same ball and chain but now his eyes are tightly shut. "This is a traditionally educated Third World Man" we are told. In the last picture the peasant has got the ball and chain off his leg and is throwing it at a bloated, pin-striped top-hatted capitalist. The caption reads: "This is a Third World Man educated for Freedom".[3]

At the 1975 Nairobi Assembly of the WCC, 12 delegates walked out of a debate on "education and renewal". One of the 12 was the Bishop of Truro. They walked out in protest when it was claimed that the purpose of education was to promote conflict and confrontation. The report of the debate maintained that "education in many societies is a consciously-used instrument of power designed to turn out persons who accept and serve the system".[4]

In 1970, the WCC sponsored the Education Renewal Fund (ERF) which was to encourage church leaders to undertake "educational renewal and reform". ERF provided lesson aids for teachers and organized training for teachers of religion in both day schools and churches. Between 1970 and 1973, ERF received over a million US dollars in donations from churches and government agencies. How many of those church leaders who availed themselves of ERF's teaching aids read them closely to discern their political aims?

In recent years, the WCC's view of education, basically crudely Marxist, has been given a more sophisticated dress by political educators such as Mr. Paulo Freire, author of **The Pedagogy of the Oppressed.** Mr. Freire, a Brazilian, was a professor at the University of Recife and became active in campaigns to combat peasant illiteracy. Accused

---

3. Risk. Vol. 6, No. 4, 1970, A WCC publication.
4. Ecumenical Press Service (EPS) No. 36, 9 December 1975. A WCC publication.

by the government of using education as a means of political subversion, he was put in prison. After leaving Brazil he joined the WCC in 1970 as a consultant on education. Here is an extract from a WCC publication discussing Freire's work and ideas:

" 'Teaching with Love' is the slogan of a Chilean adult education project that uses the Paulo Freire method of literacy training. In the process of learning to read the adult gains a sense of human dignity; realizes his potentiality and his creative power which can be used to transform society. 'Generative words' are selected both for their ideological content and phonetic meaning through a process of dialogue between teacher and illiterates. With these words, the adult can build new words and in so doing engage in a fruitful discussion on the socio-politico-economic-cultural situation in which he lives".[5]

Notice that in Mr. Freire's reading scheme the key words are chosen for their "ideological content". The literacy programme is thus being used as a means of indoctrinating the peasant with political ideas. This is rather as if reading schemes in our own primary schools were cleverly designed not merely to teach Janet and John to read but to turn them into urban guerillas.

Early in 1976, Mr. Paulo Freire was invited by the new Marxist government of Guinea-Bissau, (one of Portugal's former African territories), to launch a campaign to combat illiteracy among the peasants. Mr. Freire and his WCC helpers are directing the efforts of a team of teachers who have been recruited from the army. They are all former members of the PAIGC guerilla movement that overthrew the Portuguese and have all had special political training. It is not difficult to see how Mr. Freire's politically-motivated reading schemes can be put to good use by Marxist regimes trying to establish ideological control of new territories.

It is evident from all this, that what the WCC means by education has little to do with what most people understand by it. If we were to define education as the enrich-

---

5. See above, 3 p. 28.

ment of the person by the pursuit of learning, it is certain that the WCC would not agree with us. The WCC sees education solely as a means of making people aware of their political situation and showing them that they have the power to change it.

The WCC has never given its opinion on the political uses of education in Communist countries. This is surprising since those countries afford the plainest examples of political indoctrination of the young. In the USSR, Article 19 of the Fundamental Legislative Principles on National Education stipulates that one of the "ideological tasks" of secondary school education shall be "the formation in the younger generation of a Marxist-Leninist world-view and the inculcation of socialist internationalism . . ." In Communist countries, where every citizen is expected to toe the ideological line, education can never be the means of encouraging independent and questioning thought. As Professor Noah has pointed out, the elimination of illiteracy in the USSR has done nothing to liberate people's minds. "Rather, mass literacy was used to ensure that the ideas of the dominant ideology received the widest publicity. Universal primary and secondary education under Communism has proved to be a splendid instrument for the inculcation of an intensely narrow view of the world and the Soviet Union's place in it".[6] This is not surprising since Lenin himself was contemptuous of the liberal idea of education and wrote:

"In general, as you probably know, I do not have much sympathy for the intelligentsia, and our slogan 'liquidate illiteracy' is in no way to be interpreted as being aimed at the creation of a new intelligentsia. The purpose of 'liquidate illiteracy' is only that every peasant should be able to read by himself, without help, our decrees, orders, and proclamations. The aim is completely practical. No more".[7]

The WCC might be expected to condemn the use — or rather misuse — of education to secure ideological con-

---

6. **Problems of Communism**, Sept-Oct. 1973, p. 73.
7. **Lenin**. Robert Conquest. Fontana ed. 1972 p. 29.

formity; it seems to contradict WCC goals of "liberation" and "humanization". But while education in the West is denounced as elitist and class-ridden, education in Marxist states passes without comment. The WCC's support for the work of Mr. Paulo Freire suggests that it does not object to education being used for political indoctrination **in principle:** it is only when the "wrong" politics are being promoted that it objects.

In its attack on the values of Western education, the WCC relies heavily on the Marxist philosophy of the class struggle. Yet this is a very questionable dependence for a body that claims to be Christian. Should Christians try to change society by stirring-up antagonism between classes? If this is to be done through education, it will mean that the schools will become the battleground for class war. Instead of educating children to take their place in existing society, the WCC would teach them to believe in the necessity of "radical" social and political change — in other words, the revolution. We shall be encouraged to disparage academic achievement for, as the WCC says, we must question "whether the training of the few who obtain these skills should be at the expense of the many who do not".[8] And if existing society is as wicked and unjust, as we are told, it would be immoral to encourage school-leavers to seek to profit from it by getting a good job and pursuing personal advantage. Not only should we discourage the idea of working to perpetuate such a society but we shall scorn any sense of duty or obligation to it, the WCC implies.

Such a campaign of psychological subversion, which is now being waged by Marxists in Western schools, engenders hatred of the "system" and hostility to those who are believed to represent it. That is a heavy price to pay for the conjectural good that may result from any "new" socialist society. The Marxist revolutions that have already taken place in Russia and elsewhere suggest that the hatred and violence of the revolution are forces which, once awakened, are not so easily allayed. They stay on after

---

8. See above, 4.

the revolution and produce a more unjust society than that which was overthrown.

Christians should not be deluded by visions of Utopia: they are prepared by the doctrine of Original Sin for the harsh realities of human nature. The WCC, in adopting Marxism as a convenient tool for revolutionising Western society, has also adopted the Marxist view of man. "The highest being for Man is Man himself" wrote Marx. That is an estimate of man's place in the universe which is acceptable to an atheist but not to a Christian. Man cannot be the sole arbiter of his future: he has to reckon with morality and eternity and he has also to reckon with God.

Chapter III

WCC AND BLACK POWER IN BRITAIN

AT the Nairobi Assembly in 1975, Dr. Philip Potter attacked the British people for being "one of the most racist in history" and for having "established a racist system wherever they have gone in the world". Even Dr. Coggan, the benign and diplomatic Archbishop of Canterbury, was stung into defending his own country's record. He reminded Dr. Potter of the "immense contribution" which the British have made, and still are making, "in the realms of evangelism, medicine and education, to mention but three, to the less wealthy nations".[1] He was, of course, too polite to remind Dr. Potter that it was the "racist" British who enabled Dr. Potter, a West Indian, to come to Britain to take a degree in theology at London University and to stay for several more years in that "racist" country working with the Methodist Missionary Society and the Student Christian Movement.

Further light on Dr. Potter's attitude towards race is provided by a sermon he gave in St. Luke's Anglican Church in Kingston, Jamaica in November 1973. To a congregation of Protestants, Anglicans, Orthodox and Roman Catholics he said:

"We as churches are now under judgement both by events and by the fact that it has been the secular writers and politicians who have been the prophets of our time. Edward Blyden, Marcus Garvey, C. C. L. R. James, George Padmore, Aime Cesaire, Franz Fanon, Stokeley Carmichael, Malcolm X and others out of their Caribbean heritage have been prophets of black theology, i.e. they have given far more clear and powerful expression to the

---

1. *Church Times*, 12 December 1975.

true meaning of the right hand of God than churches as such".[2]

But who are these black writers and politicians whom God has chosen as his mouthpiece? Malcolm X was one of the founders of the militant Black Power movement in the USA. At an early age, he became involved in crime, both theft and the use of drugs, and shortly after the end of the Second World War he was sentenced to ten years' imprisonment. He joined the Black Muslims, an anti-white, anti-Christian Islamic revolutionary sect whose object is to set up a black separatist state in the southern USA. The Black Muslims are united under their spiritual leader, Master W. D. Fard, whom they believe to be the divine messenger of Allah. Little is known about Mr. Fard but he seems to have been a half-caste mystic who came to the USA from the East in the early 1930s. Here is an extract from one of Mr. Fard's messages to the faithful:

"God Almighty, in the person of Master Fard Muhammad, to whom praises are due for ever, has pointed the enemy out to us and now we say to you: let us unite all black people together, together under Allah, freedom, justice and equality, united under the crescent of Islam! We cannot unite under the cross of Christianity for freedom, justice and equality because they will not give it to you . . . Black men put the cross in their homes, worshipping one who came to give them life from this people, the Christian people. You ought to know that the cross is a sign of death, not a sign of life. Would you follow such people? Can you get to God worshipping the murderers of his prophets? . . . Allah came to deliver us from such wicked people, such merciless people who always have planned the destruction of their own black slaves. But he knew you white race. He knew what you would do before you were ever made a man. We — black men — made you and you did not make yourself, white race . . . I warn you my black brothers and black sisters . . . They are open enemies. They talk about what they have and what they will deprive us of. They would stop all outside wars to kill you

---

2. WCC's Ecumenical Press Service, 22 November 1973.

and me. They will openly tell you that they are prepared to slaughter you by the thousands, knowing that you don't have anything. Some of you do not have anything but a can of gasoline. He has guns. He has plenty of weapons to kill you. That is his joy. He would like to kill all black people".[3]

In 1965, a few months before he was murdered, Malcolm X visited Britain. He met Michael X and encouraged him to start a black power movement in this country. (Michael X was later convicted of murder and executed in Trinidad). In 1970, and again in 1971, the WCC made grants of money to the Malcolm X Liberation University in the USA.

Mr. Stokeley Carmichael, another of Dr. Potter's prophets of God, assumed greater prominence as an American Black Power leader after the death of Malcolm X. In 1967, he also visited Britain. Mr. Ian Greig, who has written several books on subversion and revolution, comments:

"The Black Power movement in Britain undoubtedly owes much of its inspiration to the American movement and indeed, had it not been for the visits of Malcolm X and Stokeley Carmichael, it would seem very doubtful if the movement would have made even the very limited progress it has".[4]

Mr. Carmichael's visit was so stimulating to militant black power adherents in Britain that the Home Secretary banned him from returning. The following extract from a speech he made at a negro rally in the USA in 1968 gives a fair idea of Mr. Carmichael's talent for inflaming racial passions:

"In order to stop police brutality we've got to kill some white cops. We don't have to stand and yell about it. We just organise and kill some white cops. There's not a right or wrong about killing. It's not a matter of who has the power to do so. It's more honourable to kill a honky cop than a Vietnamese . . . we have to create a feeling that the

---
3. From the American Black Muslim paper **Muhammed Speaks**, 2 November 1973.
4. Ian Greig, **Today's Revolutionaries**, p. 40, London, 1970.

killing of a honky cop is justified in the black community. Whenever a white cop is killed, no black man should speak out against it".[5]

Just before Mr. Carmichael's visit to Britain, Michael X had made a highly inflammatory speech at Reading. He was charged with inciting racial hatred and sentenced to a year's imprisonment. At the trial, it was alleged that he had advocated the killing of white people and had said :

"The first time I killed a white man, I thought about it. A book I read said that one wouldn't be able to sleep at night. I slept well that night". Michael X was president of a black power movement called the Racial Action Adjustment Society (RAAS). Its full-time organiser was Mr. Roy Sawh, an Indian who came to Britain from British Guiana in 1959 and later spent two years in Soviet Russia. For some time Michael X's London flat was used as the headquarters of RAAS. In 1969 when the WCC held a "Consultation on Racism" at Notting Hill, one of London's immigrant areas, Mr. Roy Sawh made such a violent speech that he was interrupted by the co-chairman, the Archbishop of Canterbury: Dr. Ramsey later apologised for having done so. In 1971, the WCC, quite undeterred by Mr. Sawh's militancy, (perhaps encouraged by it), made a grant of £1,000 to a proposed Free University for Black Studies in London. The promoter of this "university" was Mr. Roy Sawh. He considered himself insulted by the grant since, in his view, the WCC merely paid lip-service to improving race relations and he therefore returned the cheque.

The WCC's 1969 Consultation on Racism was an important step in setting up the Programme to Combat Racism (PCR) which dispenses grants to African terrorists and black power groups in Britain and the USA. Notting Hill was doubtless chosen as the meeting place for its symbolic value: in 1958 violent race riots had occurred there. The Consultation itself was a somewhat riotous affair. Dr. Eugene Carson Blake, who was at that time general secretary of the WCC, said he wanted it to be more of an

---

5. Ibid. Quoted by Greig on p. 14.

"event" than an academic meeting: he must have been well satisfied with it since the chairman, Dr. George McGovern, the left-wing Democratic senator, was quite unable to keep order. There were frequent interruptions from uninvited black power militants. One of these leapt to the platform and demanded millions of dollars in compensation for ills done to negroes by white men. "We shall have freedom, he said, "or your Christian society, your Christian banks, your Christian factories, your Christian universities, and your fine churches will be levelled for ever." Pauline Webb, vice-chairman of the WCC, reporting on the Consultation said, "The voice of God happened to us . . . We became aware of the voice of God's judgement on the evil of white racism allied with political and economic and military power". But the WCC did not, it seems, become equally aware of the evil of **black** racism. On the contrary, it was busily engaged in providing itself with the means of **encouraging** black power.

One of the Consultation's seven recommendations was:
"All else failing, support resistance movements, including revolutions, aimed at the elimination of political and economic tyranny which makes racism possible". No doubt most churchmen assumed that this was aimed at the white governments of southern Africa. But the WCC intended something much more fundamental and far-reaching than the overthrow of the surviving white regimes in Africa, necessary though that was. It proposed striking at the heart of white racism — the USA and the old imperial powers of Europe. Racism, explained the WCC, in one document, "is the coincidence of an accumulation of wealth and power in the hands of the white peoples, following upon their historical and economic progress during the past 400 years . . . People of different colour suffer from this racism in all continents . . ." There follows a list of such peoples ending with "coloured immigrants and students in the UK".[6] In the eyes of the WCC, these immigrants had precisely the same status in white society

---

6. Elisabeth Adler, **A Small Beginning**, p. 87, WCC, 1974.

as the black majorities in South Africa and Rhodesia: they were the victims of racist attitudes that would always prevent them attaining social equality. We have already heard Dr. Potter condemning British society as "racist". In 1973, on the occasion of the WCC's 25th anniversary he said: "If there is one message that has come from the WCC's work on development and racism it is that we now know just how deeply we are all implicated in the economic and political structures which maintain racism and underdevelopment. All of us, including the churches, are part of repressive systems whether in southern Africa or the so-called affluent societies where there is little genuine participation of people in the life of their societies. If we really claim to love our fellow men can we really go on supporting structures which dehumanise and oppress?" If violent movements in Southern Africa could legitimately be supported by the churches on the grounds that they were opposing racism, why not also in Britain?

In 1970, the newly created Programme to Combat Racism (PCR) announced its first batch of grants. Most of the beneficiaries were African terrorist movements but £3,500 went to the West Indian Standing Conference (WISC) an immigrant group in Britain. This was to be the first of several grants to similar groups in this country. The WISC had been founded in 1958 for the worthwhile purpose of discussing immigrants' problems, but, already by 1961, there was a noticeable change of policy — a swing away from the attempt to cultivate friendly relationships with the host society and a rejection of the idea of integration. There was instead a movement towards racial separation and black power. In 1966, WISC published a study by Mr. Joseph Hunte, one of its leaders, entitled **Nigger Hunting in England?** The writer charged the police with being "malicious and sometimes exceptionally hostile". In 1968 the **Guardian** newspaper reported that WISC "believed that the police did not intend to treat black people fairly and impartially and that liaison on the part of the police was simply to whitewash and hoodwink the community and especially the black community into believing that the police are the fairest in the world".' The grant was made to WISC "to promote solidarity among the black community with a view to creating a strong grass roots black power base which could effectively protect them and thus combat racism": those are the WCC's own words.

In 1971, came the grant of £1,000 to the Black "University" which has already been mentioned. In 1973, there was a grant of £3,500 to the Institute of Race Relations. The Institute had been started in 1958 as a non-political, unofficial research body. Its Council was graced by, amongst others, such liberal academics as Sir Robert Birley and Lord Boyle, City men Mr. David Sieff and Mr. Harry Oppenheimer and two professionals of the race relations industry, Mr. Mark Bonham Carter and Mr. Dipak Nandy. In 1963, the Institute commissioned a survey of race relations in Britain. The money was provided by the Nuffield Foundation and five years later the massive report — over 800 pages — was published.

But although the Institute started out with pretensions to academic detachment and political innocence, it was soon to go the way of all groups in the race relations field. There were those on its staff to whom the Institute's moderation was a cover for weakness and its political neutrality a cowardly refusal to commit itself. They wanted the Institute to do something more than provide documentary comment on a worsening race situation: they wanted the Institute to act — on the side of the immigrants. In 1973, tension between the Council and this radical Marxist faction became more strained. A vote by members of the Institute forced most of the Council to resign. The radicals broke away from the now tottering Institute to form a vigorous new black power group, Towards Racial Justice. They took with them the Institute's magazine, **Race Today**. In February 1974, at a meeting in Communist East Germany, the WCC announced that the new group had been given a grant of £4,500.

---

7. Nicholas Deakin, **Colour, Citizenship and British Society**, p. 254, London, 1970.

Towards Racial Justice (TRJ) is led by Mr. Darcus Howe who comes from Trinidad. He is the son of an Anglican clergyman and a self-confessed Marxist. What are the aims of TRJ? There is no attempt to conceal them. "Our political aim is to assist the black population to manifest its revolutionary potential for the development of the working class as a whole . . . black people have moved from the role of victim to protangonist, and this change in their role will be one of the most potent forces of revolutionary change in Britain. Black people have already displayed their revolutionary potential in a spate of strikes by Asian workers, and by the readiness of young West Indians to resist police harassment and intimidation and to refuse to be hewers of wood and drawers of water for British capitalists".[8]

According to Mr. Darcus Howe, the WCC grant was intended as financial support for TRJ's magazine, **Race Today,** which Mr. Howe edits. The magazine's editorial in January 1974 stated: "Our task is to record and recognize . . . the revolutionary potential of the black population". The magazine is dedicated to what it calls "the black struggle" and regards any effort towards racial harmony as a betrayal. As well as being aggressively racist, the journal is also militantly Marxist: it regards the police force, the schools, parliament and all official public institutions as instruments of ruling class oppression. **Race Today** is aimed chiefly at West Indian immigrants but sometimes includes features about Asians.

Its issue for July/August 1976 is typical. Its cover bears a picture of some unsmiling British policemen above a headline 'Up Against The Police'. The editorial begins: "What we in the West Indian community have established beyond any doubt is the attitude that we are not going to allow police officers to do as they please without offering a full-blooded resistance". It goes on to comment on the fact that the recent police campaign to encourage black immigrants to join the police force resulted in not a single new recruit. "For us in **Race Today,** the West Indian com-

---

8. **Daily Telegraph,** 24 April 1974.

munity had succeeded in turning the police campaign into one of the most powerful political statements we have made since we have been in this country. We are saying in fact that as a community we would take no part in assisting the white establishment in maintaining their law and order over the rest of society". By giving publicity to the frequent clashes between police and blacks, it says, "we have shattered the myth of the nice British bobby . . . we are now left with the task of organising our forces . . . to get the police off our backs . . . That is our aim . . ." In pursuit of this aim it advocates "mass organisation, based on those who are directly involved in the struggle . . . students, unemployed youth and parents . . . it is possible to launch such an organisation in every black community up and down the country". Elsewhere in the same issue, we are told that "it is through these mass organisations that the strength and power of the wageless and other sections can be disciplined into a fighting force".

Another page in the same issue is headlined 'How The Police Operate'. It begins: "What then are the experiences of young blacks at the hands of police officers? If we could attribute a general strategy to the police then it can be described as harass, attack and disperse . . . it is a recurring story of truncheons drawn, excessive brutality and racist abuse." The same page alleges that "for the police any one who is wageless is a thief or about to steal". On the opposite page is a reference to "the methods used by the police to attack and demoralise the wageless". On yet another page, after saying that "street fighting between young blacks and the police has become commonplace in the black communities throughout Britain", the magazine draws the predictable Marxist conclusions: "We are faced with a developing political movement of black people against the police and the movement is national in scope. The nature of this movement has to be spelled out . . . We have to be clear about the forces involved in this movement and the nature of those forces ranged against us . . ."

In the same month that saw the publication of that issue of **Race Today**, the West Indians of Notting Hill held their annual carnival. It attracted some 200,000 immigrants. Beginning with a few arrests for pick-pocketing, violence between blacks and police erupted and in the street battles that followed 325 policemen were injured. It cannot be said that **Race Today** was unprepared for the violence: in its April editorial it spoke of attempts to move the carnival to a safer area. We have no political power admitted the magazine, "but we have a power all our own. We have the support of thousands of West Indians in the community and throughout Britain. We have, too, the capacity to mobilise them against any attempt to push us around. It is the responsibility of the authorities not to provoke the black community lest the tradition of black militancy in Notting Hill", a reference to the riots in 1958 and 1971, "has to again assert itself. The organising committee is not without responsibility in this matter either. We aim to hit the streets of Notting Hill for Carnival 1976".

After the carnival riots, the September editorial described them as "a political victory" and a "crushing defeat of a well-deployed police army". On another page we are told that "the Metropolitan Police made attempts to undermine our carnival. They were repaid in kind. Several hundred young blacks inflicted a military defeat on a military organisation. The police came prepared for a confrontation and got it". And the editorial ends with what seems very like a promise of further riots: "Until and unless British society ensures that this growing section of the population gets what it needs and demands on its own terms, it will have no option but to turn up, looking for the main chance at public gatherings. Especially those gatherings which they feel are demonstrations of their community's social power".

It may be thought remarkable that a supposedly Christian body such as the WCC should give money and encouragement to a group that has such a contempt for civil peace as TRJ. After the first grant of £4,500 in 1974, it gave them £7,000 in 1975 and a third grant of £15,000 in 1976. But perhaps it is not so remarkable. Dr. Potter, as we have seen, regards the British people as "one of the most racist in history". Perhaps the WCC believes that the devil of white racism can only be cast out by the devil of black racism?

It should be of special concern to British Christians that responsibility for these grants is shared by the WCC with the **British** Council of Churches. When a group in Britain applies to the WCC for a grant, the WCC asks the BCC to investigate the group and then, if it is satisfied, recommend that the grant is made. In doing this, the BCC must use the criteria laid down by the WCC for this purpose. These state quite clearly that grants shall only be made to groups that **combat** racism and not to "welfare organisations that alleviate the effects of racism": that grants should aim at "strengthening the organisational capability of racially oppressed people": that they should "support organisations that align themselves with the victims of racial injustice and pursue the same objectives": and finally that in countries like Britain, grants should go only to groups that are so deeply committed politically that they cannot get help from other sources.

There is nothing in these criteria that either forbids or even makes it difficult to approve grants to groups such as TRJ. There is nothing to suggest that a group that uses violence or incites other people to violence will be disqualified from receiving grants. These criteria were adopted by the WCC in 1970 and it is now rather late in the day for some churchmen to attempt to dissociate themselves from the WCC's support of violent revolutionary movements. "I speak as one who supports the Programme to Combat Racism except in so far as it condones the use of violence to achieve its ends" said the Archbishop of Canterbury at the WCC's 1975 Nairobi Assembly. Dr. Coggan makes the mistake of supposing that PCR is inspired by a gentle English liberalism.

'Churchmen Uneasy on Gift to Black Power Group' was the headline in the **Guardian** of 25 April 1974. Most national papers carried similar reports of the controversy that had broken out at a BCC meeting in London about the grant to TRJ. The Revd. Harry Morton, **Methodist** general secretary of the BCC, thought that the grant was justified on the grounds of freedom of speech and freedom of publication. But he added that he didn't agree with **Race Today's** policy "which often seemed to stir up racial hatred rather than allay it".[9] Nevertheless, he defended the ight to publish it. Dr. David Russell, secretary of the Baptist Union, countered by saying that the same argument could be used to justify a grant to the Communist newspaper **The Morning Star**. Fr. Hugh Bishop, who was then the chairman of the BCC's race relations department, defended the grant with the curious argument that "a growing number of young black people in Britain felt frustrated and needed an outet".[10] But what sort of an outlet? Race riots?

The grant to TRJ shocked some of the WCC's staunchest allies. The Bishop of Bristol, a member of the WCC's Central Committee, wrote personally to Dr. Potter complaining that the journal **Race Today** was "a clearly Marxist paper" and that TRJ "was most unwisely put on the list if you want to pay any heed to responsible people engaged in race relations in Britain".[11] But even Dr. Tomkin's pleas were of no avail. Revd. Harry Morton admitted at the BCC meeting that when the WCC asked the advice of the BCC's race relations unit, "the Unit, with my encouragement, supported TRJ's application". It should be noticed that the British churches had no opportunity of discussing this most controversial of grants before the BCC gave its approval. Yet the BCC claims — in title at least — to be in some degree representative of the British churches. The grant was announced by the WCC in February 1974 but it was not until the press reports of the BCC meeting in April that British church members — and the British people generally — were aware of what had been done.

Two months later, in a debate in the Church of England's General Synod, one speaker claimed that **Race Today** described itself as a journal "dedicated to Black

---
9. **Daily Telegraph**, 24 April 1974.
10. **Times**, 25 April 1974.
11. Bishop Kenneth Sansbury, **Combating Racism**, p. 53, BCC,

Power and the overthrow of the capitalist system". But the rumblings of debate soon died down to be revived in a milder form in the autumn of 1975 when the second grant to TRJ was announced. 'Controversial Race Body Backed by BCC" was the headline in the Anglican **Church Times** 3 October. The WCC had been in some doubt about making a further grant to TRJ and had once again asked the advice of the BCC. The BCC appointed a committee to review the matter and consult with the leaders of TRJ. The BCC was particularly concerned to prove to the WCC that TRJ met all the requirements laid down in the WCC's criteria. Was, for example, TRJ more active in promoting revolution than in combating racism? Was it merely using racism as a means of arousing black immigrants to attack white society? The committee's report stated that the leaders of TRJ "were entirely open about their debt to Marxist thinking ... some of the committee were disturbed ... and concluded that the prime concern was political revolution of a kind that the churches could not support." But this was not the view of the majority which was convinced that TRJ was "visionary but pragmatic, with no narrow commitment to a particular Marxist line, e.g. Leninist or Maoist". The Committee, therefore, took the view that TRJ's primary concern was combating racism rather than revolution and that it could be approved for a grant. The WCC was given the go-ahead.

TRJ's own views, embodied in the report, are worth noting. "The British are resistant to externally induced change ... whereas in the past the British either incorporated change into their existing structures or destroyed the challenge of change, neither of these processes is possible in dealing with black Britain. The first objective of TRJ was, therefore, to preserve the separate identity of the black community lest it be destroyed by the host community. The second objective was to change British society".[12] TRJ, it seems, had not repented of any of its political aims.

---

12. Quoted in **Vision One**, November 1975, a BCC monthy paper.

In the course of its investigations, the committee discovered that there was very little support in the black community for **Race Today's** aggressively Marxist approach to political and social issues. A further point, made by Bishop David Sheppard, was that "the majority of black community leaders would not take the view that the editorials of **Race Today** take". Disappointingly, the committee did not make the further discovery that **Race Today** speaks neither for the black community at large nor for responsible black leaders but for a tiny coterie of black and white intellectuals.

In August 1976, the WCC announced a second grant of £2,500 to the Institute of Race Relations and a third grant — the largest yet — to Race Today Collective (RTC), which TRJ was now calling itself. The Revd. Elliott Kendall, director of the BCC's Community and Race Relations Unit, welcomed the new grants "to organisations in Britain and elsewhere which are seeking to combat racism. Of course" he warned "this action, like similar decisions in the last six years, is controversial and will be misunderstood. It is also likely to be misrepresented. Christians are naturally hesitant about becoming involved with those who are reluctantly taking violent measures against racial oppression. Some of these grants involve that dilemma".[13] Mr. Kendall described the grants as "controversial": in the event they produced no controversy in either Church or secular papers. Within a few days of the grants being announced, the Notting Hill riots began. People watched on their television screens as police defended themselves with dustbin lids and milk crates against bottles and bricks thrown by coloured mobs. The smooth cliches of the professionals of the race relations industry were being translated into a frightening reality. It was also a sobering reality: for what arguments could be found to convince the British people that justice was on the side of the rioters or that such violence could legitimately be supported by the Churches?

---

13. Quoted in report in **Church Times**, 27 August 1976.

The BCC's responsibility for the encouragement of black power in Britain was deepened in April 1976 by the publication of its working party's report entitled **The New Black Presence in Britain: A Christian Scrutiny**. It had an introduction by Bishop David Sheppard and a preface by Revd. Harry Morton in which he described the report as "an invitation to Whites to engage with angry and alienated Blacks — to see ourselves as others see us". The Church of England Newspaper announced the report with a front-page headline 'Racist Church in a Racist Society' — a fair summary of the report's message.

The report is unconventional in that seven out of 21 pages are devoted to the individual views of the West Indian who chaired the working party, Mr. Gus John. In his preface Revd. Harry Morton says "I disagree with Gus John's prognosis about our society. But I recognise that the challenge of the black presence will not go away". This recalls his earlier statement that he disapproved of much of the magazine **Race Today**, but nevertheless thought it ought to be published. Mr. John's own views are, in fact, indistinguishable from those of **Race Today** and when he wants to illustrate the attitudes of young black people to white society he quotes one-and-a-half pages from an issue of the magazine.

According to Mr. John, ours is "essentially a racist society" that has deliberately confined the black immigrant to decaying urban areas "rumbling with the conflict generated by dispossessed groups aspiring towards a more humane way of life". Immigration legislation is "repressive" and the first attempt to control immigration — the Immigrants' Act of 1962 — "ushered in the era of institutional racism". The social services are specially designed to operate to the disadvantage of the blacks; and the police, implementing Government policy, have tried "to prove to the black people that they did not belong and had no rights".

In a society which has institutionalised racism, says Mr. John, "community relations" is "a downright humbug" serving only to enable "the oppressive system to continue the pretence that there is genuine concern about our situation as a racially oppressed minority". Integration in such a society is out of the question. "To wish to integrate with that which alienates and destroys you, rendering you less than a person, is madness." What, then, does the black man do? Does he join the host society and attempt to work for change from within? "To accept the challenge to join it and change it from within . . . is double madness", concluded Mr. John.

Having shut just about every door that could open onto a future for the black man in a white society, Mr. John's essay disintegrates into irrelevant denunciations of capitalist exploitation of the Third World and appeals to the black population of Britain to join in the struggle for "the eventual liberation of the black peoples of the world". He never does quite explain how the blacks in Britain are to liberate themselves from our "oppressive culture". But it is difficult to avoid concluding that the road that Mr. John has chosen — that of black power and Marxism — leads inevitably to race riots and violent revolution. If that is what the future holds, the BCC and the WCC must take their share of the responsibility for having promoted such profoundly un-Christian causes.

Two months after the publication of this BCC report, racial violence suddenly flared up in Southall, an area on the fringe of London settled by Sikhs. The murder of 18-year-old Mr. Gurdip Singh Chaggar by white youths resulted in large and angry demonstrations by Asians and a call by Asian leaders for squads of Asian vigilantes to patrol the streets. A few days later, Revd. Harry Morton, stirred by this menacing situation, addressed the churches: "In the BCC we believe that the situation is dangerous and that further deterioration could harm race relations for a long period ahead . . . there is a particular responsibility on those concerned with the mass media, to see that reporting does not stimulate and anticipate violence . . . Many people are rightly alarmed by the rapid deterioration in race relations in certain areas during the last weeks. Mutual goodwill and harmonious relations which had been built up painfully over a long period have in some instances been put at grave risk".[14]

Mr. Morton seemed remarkably indifferent to the beam in his own eye. Did it never occur to him that the support given by the WCC and the BCC to black power in Britain had already put "harmonious race relations" at "grave risk"? And did not the hatred and resentment engendered by the magazine **Race Today** make "mutual goodwill" impossible and also "stimulate and anticipate violence"? Mr. Morton's platitudes were strikingly at variance with the necessary consequences of the BCC's policy of supporting militant black power in Britain. The gap between fantasy and reality had widened. Either Mr. Morton had not noticed it, or had, but hoped that others wouldn't.

Since the first edition of this book, the WCC has made two further grants to Race Today Collective, or Towards Racial Justice as it used to be known: £17,500 in 1977 and £6,500 in 1978. More importantly, however, it has now become clear that not only the World Council of Churches but also the **British** Council of Churches has for some years been funding this same black power group. This was quite unexpected since the author, in his researches for this book, had found no trace of any admission that the BCC, in addition to the WCC, were also financing RTC. Had it been a carefully kept secret? If so, the Bishop of Bath and Wells let the cat out of the bag in 1978 when, in the April issue of his Diocesan News, he mentioned the BCC's "modest financial backing (£2,000 p.a.)" for RTC's magazine **Race Today**. He went on to say: "The BCC takes the view that it is right to help a minority group who could not otherwise afford it with the production of a newspaper, even though member churches of the BCC and indeed individual Christians will often be totally opposed to the stuff that is printed there. Certainly the mainly West Indian producers of **Race Today** are loud in their praise of the Churches' concern for them — and then in the next

---

14. **Vision One,** July/August 1976.

breath they violently denounce the white people of Wolverhampton or Southall or wherever it is, in no uncertain Marxist terms".

The author subsequently learned that the Bishop was mistaken about the amount of the annual grant — it is, in fact, £3,000. The grant is made by the BCC's Community and Race Relations Unit (CRRU) whose chairman is Miss Pauline Webb, the only British member of the WCC's Executive Committee and the WCC's leading propagandist in Britain. CRRU makes grants to many immigrant groups and one of the sources of its income is the charity Christian Aid which donates about £80,000 a year to CRRU. Some of this money is for CRRU's running costs and the rest is to give away to deserving causes. But to what causes and how deserving are they? The BCC was unhelpful when the author asked for details of the grants:

"Grants made by the Board of CRRU are not public information. Many of the local projects, which are assisted by the Board, do not wish to be subject to the risk of national publicity. The Council has no wish to embarrass them when lives may be endangered and property threatened. I am, therefore, unable to supply you with the information you have requested about CRRU grants." RTC may not be the only Marxist black power group on CRRU's list of beneficiaries. If there are others it is not surprising that they wish to avoid "the risk of national publicity". And what sort of race relations work is done by groups whose lives may be endangered by publicity? In spite of the fact that the list of beneficiaries remains secret, the General Synod of the Church of England voted in November 1978 to give £700,000 to CRRU over the next seven years. The money is to go into CRRU's grants fund. It is altogether laudable to give to deserving causes but when the "cause" is unknown, it is surely an irresponsible use of Church money. Nor can it be urged that the Church can have confidence in the BCC's ability to dispense the money wisely: the fact that money is already being given to RTC is sufficient proof to the contrary.

In November 1977, Mr. Louis Chase, one of the West Indian organisers of the Notting Hill Carnival, preaching in a London Methodist church, criticised the BCC for giving its support to "distorted and irresponsible leadership within the Black community". The black groups that get support from the BCC, he said, "interpret the struggle as making as much mischief as possible — a view which would commend itself to the Socialist Workers' Party, which wants to use blacks as cannon fodder for their revolution".[15] That such criticisms are voiced by a leader of the West Indian immigrants is a measure of how far the BCC has gone in its encouragement of dangerously extremist groups.

---

15. **Times,** 21st November 1977.

Chapter IV

WCC, SOVIET UNION AND HUMAN RIGHTS

IN February 1972, Metropolitan Nikodim of the Russian Orthodox Church visited New Zealand for a WCC meeting. When he stopped off at Brisbane, Bishop Constantine of the Orthodox Church in exile, refused to see him. "It would", he said, "be an act of disloyalty to millions of Orthodox Christians who suffer for their faith. It would be a public reproach to all who suffer today in the Soviet Union because of the suppression of religion—Orthodox, Protestant, Catholic, Jewish, Muslim and others".

Instead of Bishop Constantine there were 70 demonstrators carrying placards. One of them, translated, read: "Where is your brother Talantov?" The **Brisbane Sunday Mail** reported that this placard made Nikodim angry. Mr. Boris Talantov had died just a year before in a Soviet prison camp. So had his father before him. They were both faithful, if outspoken, members of Nikodim's Church. Each had died for his faith. Yet at press conferences all round the world, Nikodim had so often said that there was no religious persecution in Soviet Russia.

At the age of 31, Nikodim became the youngest bishop in Christendom: he had a decided talent for self-advancement. A year later, he was given charge of the Foreign Relations Department of the Moscow Patriarchate and thus became one of the most powerful men in the Russian Orthodox Church. It was largely due to his efforts that the Soviet Government ended its hardline opposition to the "ecumenical movement". In 1961, a six-man team of Russian Orthodox Church (ROC) delegates attended a WCC Assembly for the first time: the team was led by Nikodim.

It is often said that the WCC's pro-Soviet bias in foreign affairs is dictated by the presence of delegates from the Soviet bloc. Voting figures on major political issues prove that this it not so: the majority would vote that way even if the Soviet bloc delegates were not present. In 1961, when a vote was taken on whether to admit the Soviet delegation, there were only three votes against. The excessive tedium of WCC assemblies has always been due to the fact that there is no strong pro-Western opinion, hence there is never any real debate. The ROC did not join the WCC to hi-jack it: that was not necessary. The WCC was already going in a direction that suited the Soviet Government admirably. It is, nevertheless, true that since 1961 a hard-core of pro-Soviet opinion has formed in the WCC's powerful policy-making Central Committee. Made up of a coalition of Eastern Orthodox delegates and members from the Third World countries, this grouping is always ready to veto any criticism of Soviet tyranny while freely indulging its own anti-Western prejudices. Even the Bishop of Bristol, a member of the Committee and a leading apologist for the WCC, admitted in a letter to the Anglican **Church Times** of 7 September, 1973 that 58% of the Committee was hostile to the West. That same year there was striking evidence of the fact when only about a third of the Committee's 120 members were prepared to sign a telegram appealing to Mr. Brezhnev to allow Solzhenitsyn to live in Moscow with his wife and children!

It is manifestly true that representatives of the Russian Orthodox Church when travelling abroad are expected by their government to toe the Party line and, when necessary, act as a mouthpiece for Soviet foreign policy. The ROC delegates to the WCC are no exception to this. Bishop Beky, of the Hungarian Reformed Church in America, was one of the few who opposed the admission of the ROC delegates to the WCC in 1961. In a speech to the Assembly, referring to "the many thousands of martyrs of modern persecutions" in the ROC, he continued, "the official representatives of the ROC will use this platform for political purposes contrary to the true spirit of that church and will endeavour to represent the views of their government, based upon the principles of an atheist materialism and an undemocratic system of one-party dictatorship".[1]

Looking back over the past 15 years of the WCC's activity, there can be no reasonable doubt that the Bishop's predictions have been amply fulfilled. Like a parent who favours one child at the expense of the other, the WCC has persistently scolded and chastised the Western world for its alleged wrongdoing while at the same time it has failed even to notice the far worse misdemeanours of Soviet Russia. The ROC delegation, backed by its Third World sycophants, must not be blamed for merely reinforcing and manipulating attitudes already present in the WCC. The WCC is staffed by professional ecumenists and intellectuals who exhibit all the symptoms of a sickness which is general in the West. Consumed by post-imperial guilt, they are convinced that the West can only expiate its crimes by humbling itself before its former victim, the Third World, and its future destroyer, Communism. Politics for them is an elaborate suicide for which Christianity affords a moral justification. The affluence of the West is an offence to them: they will not be content until the West has penitentially stripped itself of its wealth and its armaments. And they believe that it has a moral duty to do both.

But morality for the WCC is only a means to a political end. Like the practised elder statesman, the WCC knows when to strike a grand moral posture, but it also knows that if it is to achieve its purposes, morality will have to be kept in its place.

At its first general assembly in Amsterdam in 1948, the WCC declared: "It is part of the mission of the Church to raise its voice of protest wherever men are the victims of terror, wherever they are denied such fundamental rights as the right to be secure against arbitrary arrest, and

---
1. Report of the Third Assembly of the WCC, SCM Press, 1952, p. 14.

wherever governments use torture and cruel punishments to intimidate the consciences of men".²

It was brave and altogether praiseworthy of the WCC to set itself that task in the middle of the 20th century — an age of concentration camps and totalitarian regimes. Should not the Church be the voice of the voiceless, helper of the helpless? Should not the Church raise itself above the clash of rival ideologies to speak on behalf of the victims of political oppression? Most certainly it should. How has the WCC discharged its self-imposed task?

In 1973, the 120 members of the WCC's Central Committee met in Geneva. These men represent the churches that are members of the WCC. They met to discuss the theme of 'Violence, Non-Violence and the Struggle for Social Justice'. They drew up a list of examples of oppression and discrimination from the following countries and areas: South Africa, Latin America, Northern Ireland, the Middle East and the USA. In South Africa, we are told, "many Christians support a government representing a white minority that imposes its will upon a black majority by coercion, threats and frequently overt violence, to protect their privileged status . . ." In Latin America, violence shows itself, "through oppressive acts such as unjust imprisonment of opponents by the government, torture, censorship of the communications media and through economic exploitation backed by political power". The question that millions of Latin Americans face, we are told, "is how to overthrow the forces perpetuating this situation". In the section on the USA, there is a reference to its "massive, obvious violence" in Vietnam and its "economic domination and political interventions, sometimes openly violent, in Latin America". It goes on to say that the civil rights and other protest movements in the USA had sometimes been forced to adopt violence "against a systematic oppression armed with weapons both brutal and subtle".³

---

2. Report on The First Assembly of the WCC, SCM Press, 1949, pp. 79-80.
3. **Violence, Non-Violence and the Struggle for Justice,** WCC, 1973.

In this list of examples of oppression and violence not one was drawn from a Communist country. The WCC seemed to have overlooked the fact that several hundred million people in Soviet Russia and Eastern Europe are kept in place by electrified fences, trip-wire operated mines and guard dogs that Russia keeps a slave population of over a million in labour camps, living on starvation rations and forced to do long hours of heavy labour. The WCC conveniently turns a blind eye to the fact that Soviet citizens are under constant surveillance by the secret police and are punished for any deviation from the ideological norm; that there is no free press or radio since every word that is made public must first be approved by the state censor, and that its citizens lack the basic right of religious freedom — a man may be sent to a labour camp for holding a prayer meeting in his home and a mother may be forcibly deprived of her children for teaching them their prayers.

The absence of any examples from the Communist world was noticed by at least one of the members of the Central Committee, Professor Olle Engstrom of Sweden. He suggested that there should be some reference to the suppression of human rights in Communist countries. Delegates from Communist countries rose one after another to deny that there was any such denial of rights. The Professor's suggestion was voted on and was heavily defeated: only two out of the 120 members supported him, 26 others abstaining.

This WCC meeting in 1973 clearly illustrates the political bias which has characterised the WCC's policies in international affairs for the past 25 years. It may be fairly summarised as anti-Western and pro-Communist. It expresses itself in the use of a double-standard of international morality and selective moral indignation: injustices in Western countries are highlighted as targets for vehement censure while worse injustices in Communist countries are ignored. Injustice and oppression are not condemned **impartially** wherever they occur as afflictions of the human spirit but only if it is politically advantageous to do so. Such judgements are political not moral, and in the hands of the WCC moral censure has become a political weapon. Yet at its Utrecht meeting in 1972, the WCC had rededicated itself "to assist in the implementation of human rights wherever they are being violated, seeking to avoid all ideological prejudice".

If we examine some international crisis in which Western and Soviet interests have clashed, we shall find that the WCC's object is either positively to encourage Soviet Russia or, more subtly, to undermine the self-confidence of the West. The Cuban missile crisis is an example of the former. There is no doubt that the WCC regarded the USA as the aggressor. At the height of the crisis on 2 October 1962, the General Secretary of the WCC, Mr. Visser t'Hooft, issued the following statement on behalf of officers of the WCC, who had, it said, ". . . on several occasions expressed their concern and regret when governments have taken unilateral military action against other governments. The officers of the WCC consider it, therefore, their duty to express grave concern and regret concerning the action which the US government has felt it necessary to take with regard to Cuba and fervently hope that every government concerned will exercise the greatest possible restraint in order to avoid a worsening of the international tension". 1,000 delegates at the conference of the Lutheran Church in America, which was then in session, repudiated this WCC statement on the grounds that it was an attack on the government of the USA. Metropolitan Nikodim, however, of the Russian Orthodox Church, was able to write to Mr. Visser t'Hooft, "We approve your condemnation in the name of the WCC of these dangerous acts of the American government against the republic of Cuba . . ."[4] 12 days after Mr. Visser t'Hooft's condemnation of the USA an American reconnaissance plane brought back photographs of Soviet missile sites in western Cuba.

---

4. Quoted in William C. Fletcher's **Religion and Soviet Foreign Policy 1945-1970,** London. 1973.

An example of the WCC's more subtle approach to an international crisis is its carefully modulated response to the Soviet subjugation of Czechoslovakia in 1968. In July of that year, as the crisis deepened, the WCC met in General Assembly in Uppsala, Sweden. The Assembly might have been expected to give some encouragement to the "Prague Spring", particularly as Dubcek's attitude towards the Christian Churches was the most liberal since the Communist coup of 1948. But the Assembly said nothing at all about Czechoslovakia. It neither supported Dubcek nor did it reproach Soviet Russia. But it did address a unilateral request to the USA to stop the bombing of military targets in North Vietnam. An attempt to link this with a condemnation of the infiltration of South Vietnam by Communist Viet Cong terrorists was defeated. Revd. Bernard Pawley, Archdeacon of Canterbury, reported the assembly for the Anglican **Church Times**. He commented:

"And at a time when heroes in Czechoslovakia were trying at great cost and danger to step loose from the most sinister of modern tyrannies, not a word of support or protest from the WCC — an amazing double coup for the propaganda machine of the USSR".[5]

When, finally, Soviet tanks rolled into Prague, every civilised voice was raised in protest. Only the WCC remained silent. It was some weeks before it addressed a note to the Soviet government feebly remonstrating over what it described as "an ill-considered action".[6]

After the fall of Dubcek, the Churches in Czechoslovakia were subjected to hard, Stalinist persecution. Of 4,000 Catholic priests more than 500 have been banned under one pretext or another from engaging in any priestly functions, with the result that 1,600 parishes — about one third of the total — are without priests. In 1948, there were nearly 1,000 monasteries and convents in Czechoslovakia: very few exist today. In 1975, mindful of the growing severity of persecution in Czechoslovakia, an organisation

5. **Church Times**, 26 July 1968.
6. **Church Times**, 6 September 1968.

of Czech exiles called Free Czechoslovakia wrote to Dr. Philip Potter, general secretary of the WCC saying :
"We are at a loss to understand why there are no public statements or any action on your part in regard to the religious situation in countries ruled by the Communist Party. Thousands of Christians who are not free, await your word, yet you remain silent. If you have the courage to proclaim the necessity for human rights in Chile, Brazil, and Africa, why not to express the same for Czechoslovakia? Why the complete imbalance of justice on your part? Are countries under Soviet and Communist domination not equally important, and are they not worth the attention of the World Council of Churches?'

Vietnam and Korea are other areas of international tension where the WCC has pursued pro-Soviet policies. Both of these will be discussed in greater detail in later chapters. Here it is sufficient to say that the WCC opposed American intervention in Vietnam from the earliest days, and never missed an opportunity to castigate the USA for her part in the war. In Korea today the situation very closely parallels that of Vietnam in the late 1950s: a powerful Communist North threatens the South across a demilitarised zone while the Soviet Union, China and the USA wait in the wings ready to give aid to their proteges. As might be expected, the WCC has adopted the same political stance in Korea as it did in Vietnam: the South is denigrated as a corrupt and oppressive regime while the North is absolved from any criticisms. The clear implication is that the South would benefit from being defeated and taken over by the Communist North.

A blatant example of the WCC's pro-Soviet bias occurred at the end of 1975 when rival guerilla groups were fighting for possession of Angola. While the Soviet Union was organising the airlift of 10,000 Cuban troops into Angola and Communist ships were unloading hundreds of tons of arms in Luanda harbour for the Marxist MPLA, the WCC passed a resolution on Angola. The resolution

---

7. Reported in the American journal **The Remnant,** 28 October 1975.

called upon all governments "to respect the independence and territorial integrity of Angola and to withdraw all military units and to stop the supply of arms." It declared that "South Africa's intervention in Angola" — which had been brief and ineffectual — "has seriously reduced prospects of a peaceful solution to the problems of the area". There was no mention of either Cuba or Soviet Russia.

But it is in the field of human rights that the WCC's firm refusal to utter any criticism of Soviet Russia is most strikingly obvious. In 1972, Dr. Eugene Carson Blake, who was then general secretary of the WCC, was asked by the Reformed Churches of the Netherlands if they should engage in protests against religious oppression in Eastern Europe. Dr. Blake seemed to do his best to discourage them: "Most people in the West," he said, "have only a partial image of the life of God's people in socialist countries. They are often victims of cold-war propaganda, repeating stories from the worst period of Stalinist oppression". He went on to say that the best way of helping those in Eastern Europe was by taking our "ecumenical opportunities" seriously. "If we do not really get to know the churches in socialist countries, our expressions of critical concern become cheap and can only be understood in the countries concerned as anti-Communist, i.e. political/theological declarations." Dr. Blake ended his reply by suggesting that the Dutch protest instead about "torture in Brazil, arbitrary justice with regard to black Americans . . . Eskimos in Canada . . . Aborigines in Australia . . . Communists in Greece and liberals in Paraguay."

While Dr. Blake was giving his advice to Dutch Christians, Roman Catholics in Lithuania were protesting against their oppressive Communist government. A young Catholic doused himself in petrol and burned himself to death in public. 17,000 Catholics signed a petition to Brezhnev. Many more would have signed had the KGB not intimidated collectors on the streets and seized some of the lists. "Freedom of conscience is still absent and the Church is subjected to persecution," said the petition. It went on to say that "atheism is forcibly inculcated in

Lithuania's Soviet schools. The believing children of Catholic parents are made to speak, write and act against their conscience." When the government told the bishops to issue a pastoral letter condemning the petition, the bishops were ready to collaborate. KGB men were sent to every parish church to see that the letter was read out on Sunday morning by the priest. Not only did many priests refuse to read the letter but some published a letter condemning the treachery of the bishops.

Those priests were brave men and so were the ordinary people who signed the petition and risked the reprisals of a police state. They might reasonably expect support from a supposedly Christian international body such as the WCC. But none came. At the end of 1974, Dr. Andrei Sakharov addressed an appeal to the WCC on behalf of six imprisoned Lithuanian Catholics. He asked the WCC "to speak out in defence of the people who have been arrested for their religious beliefs". There is no evidence of the WCC breaking its habitual silence. The WCC is undoubtedly concerned about human rights: but only in certain countries. In September 1972, for example, a team of leading American churchmen returned from a visit to Uruguay. They had been sent by the WCC to investigate charges that its right-wing government was engaged in a campaign of political oppression. "There is impressive evidence," declared the team, "that, as part of the violation of human rights, both physical and psychological torture is practiced on political prisoners."

When will the WCC send such a team to Soviet Russia? It would collect even more "impressive evidence".

In 1971 the Executive Committee of the WCC met in Communist Bulgaria and ratified a new batch of grants to terrorists in Africa. Dr. Ernest Payne, a leading British Baptist, was a member of this committee and on his return to England wrote an article for the **Baptist Times** entitled 'Churchmen in Bulgaria the Beautiful'. Dr. Payne evidently liked what he saw there — from "the tens of thousands of workers . . . greeting the Party leaders by waving bunches of flowers", to the plans for building a luxury hotel near the desecrated monastery of Rila. Only towards the end of his article did Dr. Payne admit there was anything that marred this idyllic "People's Democracy". "The country is committed to an atheistic outlook and policy", he allowed, and Baptists "have long been cut off from their brethren in other lands and have had to endure many restrictions and difficulties. They are not helped by protests and intervention from outside. Their trust is in God. They believe that, as of old, slowly but surely, He is working out his purposes of mercy and renewal".[8]

Dr. Payne's reasons for opposing Western protests against Communist oppression are interesting. God is working His purpose out in Communist countries and should not be obstructed. But isn't He also working His purpose out in South Africa and Rhodesia? Why is it that in those countries man must take matters into his own hands? Why are Africans (including many non-Christians and atheists) given moral and financial encouragement to secure their basic rights by violence, but Christians under Soviet rule are abandoned and must bear their burdens passively?

But the commonest argument used by the WCC to discourage protest against Communist oppression is that, in the case of Soviet Russia, public protest is not merely useless but actually makes the victims' situation worse. This argument ignores the fact that many appeals for help have come out of Russia and Eastern Europe specifically demanding protest action in the West. Is it likely that the victims would appeal to the West for help if they knew that by doing so their sufferings would increase? On the contrary, human rights activists in those countries know that Western public opinion and the media are powerful allies in their struggle. Solzhenitsyn has revealed that at "a time extremely dangerous to me, I was shielded from the worst repressions by a defensive wall raised about me by the world's famous writers". Maximum publicity in the West can only be a source of encouragement and help to the persecuted and an embarrassment to the perse-

8. **Baptist Times**, 30 September 1971.

cutors. The Soviet Government, in its pursuit of detente with the West, cannot afford to have the damaging facts of its tyrannical rule displayed in front of Western eyes and is doubtless grateful to the WCC for its policy of silence carefully maintained for over 25 years.

Another defence used by the WCC against its critics is to claim that the Soviet Government, unlike the South African government, is more responsive to private representations than to public protest. This argument has distinct advantages for the WCC since those who use secret diplomacy do not have to render a public account of what they have, or have not, done. Yet with mounting criticism of the WCC's double standards in international affairs, it would surely be in its own interests to prove, by revealing details of private representations in the past, that it has been as zealous for human rights in the USSR as it has been in South Africa. Unhappily the WCC has not done so and it is, therefore, difficult to resist the conclusion that its claim to prefer the private rather than the public approach in dealing with the Soviet Government is merely a face-saving device.

Yet another plea of the WCC's is that protests against injustice in Russia would upset the delegates from the Soviet bloc who would then withdraw from the WCC. This is the most remarkable of the WCC's excuses. Is it an admission that the WCC is being blackmailed into silence by the Russian delegates? Or does it mean that WCC is a willing partner to a private arrangement by which these delegates agree to retain their seats in the WCC provided there is no criticism of the Soviet Union? If this is so, then the Soviet delegates enjoy a privilege of immunity that has never been extended to the delegates from South African churches. The WCC has never shown the slightest readiness to moderate its attacks on the South African government in deference to **their** presence. Indeed, in 1960, three Dutch Reformed Churches in South Africa withdrew from the WCC in protest against these attacks.

But the WCC was to get its "come-uppance". At its 1975 Nairobi Assembly, a letter from two members of the

Russian Orthodox Church, Lev Regelson and Fr. Gleb Yakunin was smuggled out of Russia and published in the assembly's daily paper. Official replies were published three days later from the Russian Orthodox delegates to the Assembly but the match had been put to the tinder. Shortly afterwards human rights in the Soviet Union were being hotly debated in the Assembly for the first time in the history of the WCC. The letter, after summarising the history of the persecution of the Church in Russia since the Revolution, goes on to discuss the WCC:

"In 1961, the Russian Orthodox Church joined the WCC. For the Russian Church that year was marked by an increasing wave of anti-religious terror and by forcible closing of churches, monasteries and theological schools everywhere. At the same time, Protestant congregations were subjected to no less brutal persecution. The 22nd Congress of the Communist Party declared that 'this generation of Soviet people will live under Communism' — and in order probably to speed up its advent, more than 10,000 Orthodox churches were closed on the territory of the USSR from 1959 to 1965.

"The believers of the Russian Church never had any particular illusions about the fact that the Moscow Patriarchate became a member of the WCC: it was an act sanctioned by the government during a period of extremely brutal persecution of religion, and obviously followed the government's own strategic aims, which had nothing to do with the task of consolidating Christian positions in the modern world.

"Nevertheless, Orthodox believers still hoped that Christian solidarity and determination to achieve genuine unity would prove stronger than the influence of anti-Christian forces; they hoped that the WCC would provide powerful support to its new member, initiate an international movement for the defence of persecuted Christianity and invite all Christians to united prayers for the suffering Church".

The writers then briefly review the wide range of WCC activities from theological dialogue to political and military affairs, adding:

"Among such a wide range of serious problems, however, the matter of religious persecution failed to occupy the place it deserves — although it ought to become the central theme of Christian ecumenism. The world did not hear the WCC raising its authoritative voice when the Russian Orthodox Church was half destroyed; that voice was not heard either even when in that vast country China, Christianity was made illegal; no indignant protest was heard from the WCC even when religion was completely crushed in Albania — and the WCC still remained silent even after a priest was shot in Albania for having baptized a baby.

"The WCC, which is composed basically of representatives of the Protestant Churches, failed to give support to the Baptists, Jehovah's Witnesses and Pentecostalists in the USSR when their believers were subjected to persecution and oppression, and particularly when they were deprived of their parental rights because of their attempts to give their own children a religious upbringing".

The letter ends with specific suggestions for those who want to help persecuted Christians. It says that "the persecutors of Christians are now extraordinarily concerned about their international reputation". Christians in the West should therefore "find ways of promoting on the appropriate level an international protest campaign against the persecutors ... If every believer would send a letter of protest once a month to the persecutors, and if at the same time he would appeal in the same spirit to public opinion in his own country, he would undoubtedly diminish considerably the fervour of the enemies of Christianity". The writers, after saying how important it is for Christians today, like the early Christians, to revere Christians who suffer for their faith, give some examples of these "confessors". They also mention the "treatment" of Christians in psychiatric hospitals describing it as "a truly diabolical assault on human personality". They end by appealing to all delegates to the Assembly "to demand a compulsory international inspection of psychiatric hospitals because it is there that we come up against a threat to mankind no less dangerous than nuclear bombs and bacteriological warfare . . . Christians all over the world must not ignore one single case of detention of dissidents or believers in psychiatric hospitals".[9]

The Regelson/Yakunin letter was a thrust at the WCC's conscience. It was the voice of oppressed Russian Christians speaking loudly and clearly to the WCC Assembly. It had the real authority of those who have suffered for their faith: Yakunin had denounced the servility of his own Church leaders in 1965 and had been debarred from his altar for doing so. Could the WCC ignore it? There was an impromptu debate in which the unwritten rule that Soviet Russia should never be publicly castigated was triumphantly broken. Metropolitan Juvenaly was heard to say that he no longer felt that he was in a Christian assembly and there were, according to a British delegate, "bullying and blustering voices, one of which was reliably reported to have come from a KGB agent masquerading as a Baptist minister, accusing the West in a terrible, offensive kind of way . . ."[10]

Eventually, in a debate on disarmament and the Helsinki Declaration, a Swiss delegate, Dr. Jacques Rossel, proposed the following: "The WCC is concerned about restrictions to religious liberty particularly in the USSR. The Assembly respectfully requests the government of the USSR to implement effectively principle number seven of the Helsinki Agreement". Dr. Ernest Payne thereupon proposed that the whole thing be sent back to committee. This was done and the following morning the new draft of Dr. Rossel's proposal was accepted: the reference to the USSR had been removed. It is worth adding that the committee included a Russian member.

---

9. Full text of letter is in **Religion in Communist Lands**, Vol. 4, No. 1, 1976, Keston College.
10. Revd. Richard Holloway interviewed on BBC's **Anno-Domini**, 14 December 1975.

One of the outcomes of that debate was that Dr. Philip Potter was to investigate what progress had been made towards religious liberty in those countries which were signatories of the Helsinki Agreement — including, of course, Soviet Russia. In August 1976, he reported to a meeting of the WCC Central Committee. Although Dr. Potter's address was lengthy, it said nothing about religious persecution in Soviet Russia or Eastern Europe. This could not have been for lack of information: the WCC had been sent several dossiers on the situation of Christians in Communist countries — one very comprehensive record from the Centre for the Study of Religion and Communism in Britain had taken two of its full-time staff three months to prepare. But Dr. Potter did find an opportunity to remind his audience that "it is essential for churches in Europe and North America to be aware of the problems created and maintained by European and American domination of other regions of the world".

The same meeting of the Central Committee, although it made no reference to oppression in Russia, passed resolutions on both Rhodesia and South Africa. The first expressed "grave concern at the continued oppression of the people of Zimbabwe (Rhodesia) by the illegal regime, the arbitrary imprisonment and detention of political leaders and others, the execution of freedom fighters, the criminal measures of collective punishment and the continued denial of human rights under the disguise of the so-called preservation of Western civilisation". The other called upon "the South African regime urgently to end violence against the oppressed majority, to recognise immediately their full human rights, to release forthwith all those imprisoned for political reasons, and to abandon apartheid; and urges all member churches in South Africa to do everything in their power to counteract the repressive violence of the regime and to demonstrate by action their solidarity with the oppressed".[11]

So, once again, the WCC had managed to silence the voice of the persecuted Christians. The Yakunin/Regelson

---

11. Ecumenical Press Service, WCC, 26 August 1976.

letter had ended with the hope that "our suggestions will not be ignored and that they will prompt the delegates to the Assembly not only to consider them but to act upon them". Many observers of church affairs had been similarly optimistic, believing that the WCC would seize this opportunity of rising above political ideology to show that it was capable of judging the nations with a genuine impartiality. All such expectations have been disappointed. The WCC has turned a granite indifference to those who suffer Communist tyranny. It has shown an inflexible opposition to those who would persuade it that it has a duty to speak on their behalf. After the Yakunin/Regelson letter, it is mere sentimentality to expect any major change in the WCC's policy either by a movement of reform from within or by a change of heart on the part of its leaders. For this reason there is now a very strong case for member churches that object to this bias withdrawing from the WCC.

There remains to consider the **moral** consequences of the WCC's failure in the field of human rights. In 1969, Mr. Anatole Levitin was arrested in Moscow on trumped-up charges of "disloyalty to the state". Mr. Levitin was a member of the Russian Orthodox Church and had written in samizdat about the persecution of Christians and dissidents. His many friends in Russia promptly sent a letter to the WCC, to the Pope and to the Ecumenical Patriarch pleading with them to protest on Mr. Levitin's behalf. Reporting this letter the Anglican **Church Times** wrote: "It is dreadful if world-wide Christendom can do nothing in effective defence of such victims of anti-religious persecution".[12]

It is indeed.
But what did the WCC do for Mr. Levitin?
It did nothing at all.
In a letter to the writer, Mr. Levitin says: "I have no information about any action taken by the WCC in connection with my arrest in 1969. So it seems that my case has not been an exception of the rule as to the WCC".

---
12. **Church Times**, 24 October 1969.

Mr. Levitin's grasp of English prepositions may be a little unsure but he has a very sound understanding of the WCC. The wastepaper baskets at the WCC's Geneva headquarters must be full of such unanswered appeals. But if Christians in Russia cannot expect to be heard by their fellow Christians in the West, to whom can they appeal? They live in a country where human rights are treated with contempt and where the victim of the ruling ideology has no defence in the courts. Their only hope lies in the Western Churches ... a hope that is doomed to disappointment. For what they do not know, is that the Western Churches, through their membership of the WCC, have already decided, as a matter of policy, to shut their ears to all such appeals and to deny that there is persecution and oppression in Soviet Russia.

It is not surprising that some Russian Christians who have come to the West are bitter about the WCC. It seems to them that the WCC is collaborating with their former persecutors. That is precisely what the WCC is doing. It is not that the WCC is fence-sitting. It is not trying to be on both sides at once, pleading the cause of the victim without upsetting friendly relations with the persecutor. The WCC is not interested in the victims of Communism, only in the victims of capitalism and white racism, and it campaigns on their behalf not out of a sense of moral duty but to advance a political cause. The WCC, by its refusal to support the victims of Communism, has revealed that its deepest commitment is political not moral. It has also deprived itself of any credibility as a Christian body since it has, as a matter of policy, consistently subordinated the imperatives of the Gospel to political ideology.

Justice and compassion demand that the WCC supports the persecuted in Soviet Russia but the WCC, in order to concentrate its critical attack upon the West, makes excuses for not doing so. As Archbishop Athenagoras, leader of the Greek Orthodox Church in Britain and a member of the WCC's Central Committee, has said, "It seems that

Caesar with his panoply has penetrated the WCC and Christ is confronted with the danger of asphyxiation".

At the opening of this chapter, I mentioned Metropolitan Nikodim who first came to the WCC in 1961 and has led the Russian delegation ever since. Nikodim has been a great success in the West: he received a United Nations' medal for peace from the hands of U Thant and in 1975, at the WCC's Nairobi Assembly, he was elected to one of the WCC's six presidential chairs. This was a considerable achievement for Soviet ecclesiastical diplomacy. Acknowledging his election he said: "The role of the Church is in giving moral support to people fighting for liberty . . . as one of the presidents of the WCC I now feel even more concern for this kind of work".

In September 1973, Nikodim and Patriarch Pimen paid an official visit to the WCC's headquarters at Geneva where they had "extensive discussions" with Dr. Philip Potter which "ranged over a number of issues of mutual interest and concern and were conducted in a friendly atmosphere". It was to this same Pimen that Solzhenitsyn addressed his now famous 'Lenten Letter' in 1972 in which he appealed to the Patriarch not to put "self-preservation and personal gain" before the Christian faith, nor to think that "earthly power is more important than heavenly power". He continued "The church is ruled dictatorially by atheists . . . the whole of Church property and the use of Church funds is under their control . . . By what reasoning is it possible to convince oneself that the planned destruction of the spirit and body of the Church under the guidance of atheists is the best way of preserving it? Preserving it for whom? Certainly not for Christ. Preserving it by what means? By falsehood?"

I have presented sufficient evidence to suggest that there is an alliance of interests between the Soviet Government, the official leaders of the Russian Orthodox Church and the WCC. The two Christian bodies, by advancing a politicised version of Christianity, have in effect made themselves the accomplices of the Kremlin. What are the consequences of this for world Christianity? Perhaps the late

Mr. Boris Talantov, whom Metropolitan Nikodim tried to silence, should answer that question. What he says of the Moscow Patriarchate is equally true of the WCC.

"The activity of the Moscow Patriarchate is directed towards using lies and false presentation of evidence to set the Christian movement in the whole world on a false course and thereby undermine it. Such, for example, was the suggestion of the Patriarchate at the Rhodes consultation of Orthodox Churches, that Christian apologetics and the ideological struggle with modern atheism should be renounced. The activity of the Moscow Patriarchate abroad is a conscious betrayal of the Russian Orthodox Church and the Christian faith. The Patriarchate appears on the world platform as a secret agent combating world Christianity".[13]

In September 1978, Metropolitan Nikodim died at the age of 49. The circumstances of his death were rather mysterious. He had attended the installation in Rome of Pope John Paul I and a few days later had a private audience with the new Pope. While they were talking in the Pope's study, Nikodim suddenly collapsed and died. The Pope was found reciting prayers beside his body. Only 24 days later the Pope himself died unexpectedly.

---

13. Quoted in Michael Bourdeaux's **Patriarch and Prophets,** London 1969, p. 331.

Chapter V

GEORGI VINS AND THE WCC

ONE swallow doesn't make a summer, runs the old adage, and there might be some who would be tempted to think that the WCC's one and only public protest on behalf of a Russian Christian indicated a change of policy. The most likely explanation of this aberration is that some kind of action was forced on the WCC by the widespread publicity given to the Mr. Vins case and by the mounting tide of criticism directed against the WCC's notorious double standards. To make a public protest on Mr Vins' behalf was, in any case, a contradiction of the WCC's official argument that the Soviet Government was more responsive to private representations than to public protest.

The occasion of the WCC's action was the arrest of the Soviet Christian, Mr. Vins in March 1974 and his subsequent trial and conviction. This was not the first time that Mr. Vins and his family had been in trouble with the authorities. His father had died in one of Stalin's labour camps and his mother, Lydia, had served a prison sentence. Mr. Vins also had been convicted before in 1966. Although details of his trial at that time had been sent to the WCC, the United Nations Commission on Human Rights, the Baptist World Alliance and other international bodies, not one of them raised a voice in his defence. One of those who signed that appeal was a Mrs. Yakimenkova, mother of seven children. She risked her life by going to Moscow and seeking out Western journalists. She was reported in the London papers as saying: "Surely someone is listening to our appeals? Surely someone will help us? Can't you tell U Thant that we have heard nothing from him?" But no one in the West was concerned about a Baptist leader in Russia who had been sentenced for his religious convictions and whose family was being systematically persecuted.

We have an eye-witness account of the 1966 trial whereas less is known about the later trial in 1975. Soviet court procedure is unlikely to have changed much since 1966 so it's worth recalling what happened when Mr. Vins and his colleague, Mr. Kryuchkov, were brought before the city court of Moscow. The two accused applied to the court for 17 witnesses in their defence but the Prosecutor refused on the grounds that the court was in a hurry and it would take too long to summon them. The trial began on 9 November at 10 a.m. and at 7 p.m. the interrogation of Mr. Vins began. Mr. Vins protested that he was exhausted and unable to concentrate on the questions being put to him. He asked for an adjournment. The Prosecutor refused: the court was in a hurry. The cross-examination went on for two hours. Whenever Mr. Vins answered, the hand-picked audience laughed and shouted and the court made no attempt to curb the interruptions.

The next day the trial resumed at 10 a.m. and went on until **one o'clock at night.** During the evening the defence was told to begin its case. They asked for an adjournment to re-draft their case in the absence of witnesses they were not allowed to call. The request was refused and they were told that if the defence did not begin there and then, the verdict would be given without hearing a defence at all. At 1 a.m. both men were sentenced to three years in labour camps. The indictments made it plain that they had been sentenced solely for their religious convictions.

Mr. Vins was put to work as a beast of burden on a railway construction gang. Half-way through his sentence, 176 Baptists signed a petition to the Soviet Government saying there was reliable information "of the intention of certain bodies to liquidate Georgi Vins through his camp conditions". It went on to say that Mr. Vins "is now physically right at the end of his tether. When he arrived at the camp he was forced to join a building brigade and had to march to work under guard five or six miles in each direction every day through rugged mountainous terrain. Although an engineer by profession, he was used as a beast of burden, hauling logs manually from the forest to construct a railway. In these conditions Vins contracted an infection which combined with physical slavery has worn him out completely and given him heart trouble. In addition, boils have appeared all over his body. On occasions he has fainted on his way to work or while on the job, but has never been exempted from work. Finally, because the work was beyond his strength, he contracted a double inguinal hernia. Yet even after this he was forced to do this hard physical labour, although it meant that his health would be irreparably broken and even his life would be endangered".

Georgi was released in 1969, re-arrested in 1970 and sentenced to a year's forced labour in a factory. In 1974, he was arrested once again. Mr. Vins was still a sick man and his plight and that of his wife and children aroused the consciences of many in the West. Numerous appeals were made to the Soviet Government to release Mr. Vins. In October, Dr. Andrei Sakharov, the Soviet physicist, appealed to the WCC to intervene on Mr. Vins' behalf. In November, Dr. Potter wrote to officials of the Soviet Government. He asked for full details of the case, for permission to have a WCC observer at the trial, and for Mr. Vins to be given full facilities for his self-defence. In January, there had still been no reply to the WCC's requests and the trial was now imminent. The WCC issued a further appeal to the Soviet Government:

"The WCC has received information that the trial of Mr. Georgi Petrovic Vins, a well-known leader of a Baptist group, is immient in his home town of Kiev, in the Soviet Union. We regret that there has been no response from the Minister of Justice of the Soviet Union to the request made by Dr. Potter in his letter dated 14 November 1974 regarding the case of Mr. Vins. The general secretary's appeal was on the basis of representation received in this matter from several persons in the USSR.

"The general secretary in his letter had asked in particular that the text of the indictment against Mr. Vins be made available, that a legal observer be allowed to follow the proceedings of the trial and that legal defence be provided according to the expressed wish of Mr. Vins.

"We understand that Mr. Vins is charged with the violation of Soviet law, in particular Article 209-1 of the Ukrainian Criminal Code. We have reason to believe on the basis of information received that the charges against Mr. Vins are made primarily because of his religious convictions and activities. In view of the commitment of the WCC and its member churches to the fundamental right of people to live according to their own chosen religious convictions, we call upon the government of the Soviet Union to contribute towards international understanding by according permission to a legal observer to attend the trial as suggested by the general secretary of the WCC".

At the end of January the trial took place and Mr. Vins was given the maximum sentence of five years in prison followed by five years of exile. The trial was just as Dickensian as the preceding one in 1966: there was the same blatant contempt for the rights of the defendant and the same cynical disregard for the rules of evidence. The Norwegian judge whom Mr. Vins had chosen as his defence counsel was barred from the courtroom. Mr. Vins' mother, Lydia, and all of his witnesses were also refused admittance to the courtroom. Part of the evidence was a sermon that Mr. Vins had delivered at a wedding in 1969 which was alleged to contain anti-Soviet remarks. The court ordered an analysis of the tape of the sermon and no such remarks were found. The Judge disallowed this evidence and ordered a further analysis. The bride who was a key witness for the defence was not allowed in court.

In view of what the WCC knew of the Soviet government's brutal ill-treatment of Mr. Vins over a period of many years, it would have been fully justified in sending a note of strong condemnation to the Soviet Government. Instead, the letter I have reproduced is mild and restrained to the point of weakness: it seeks above all to avoid giving offence. It is instructive to compare it with another appeal — this time to the British Government — made only two months later. This appeal was not on behalf of a church leader but a terrorist leader — the Revd. Sithole, president of the ZANU terrorists in Rhodesia, who had just been arrested. The appeal states that the WCC "has long deplored the increasing erosion of human rights in Rhodesia ... We have supported the courageous stand of Rhodesian church leaders ... We have protested against the detention of African leaders and the denial of political rights to opponents of the minority regime ..." Dr. Potter then turns to the execution of three African terrorists and the arrest of Sithole: ". . . these actions constitute a flagrant violation of the letter and spirit of the Lusaka Accord, and a further serious provocation of international public opinion. They can only postpone the justice we are convinced must come". The appeal ends, "We affirm our solidarity with the Zimbabwe people in their struggle for justice, liberation and self-determination, and pray that their aspirations will soon be fulfilled". In making such an aggressive approach to the British Government, the WCC is strengthened by the fact that, as it says, it has "long deplored the increasing erosion of human rights in Rhodesia" and has always "supported the courageous stand" of Rhodesia's church leaders. In the USSR, however, it has consistently ignored the erosion of human rights and the courageous stand of Christians against a militantly atheistic state. These it has dismissed as if they were an anti-Communist, cold-war fairy tale.

The refusal of the WCC to denounce the massive injustice of Communist societies is due, of course, to its belief that Western capitalist societies are wicked, corrupt and incurably selfish and are destined to be replaced by Communism which is morally superior. The WCC must, therefore, do all it can to accelerate the decline of the West and promote the interests of International Communism. In respect of this, Mr. Georgi Vins is a representative figure. The movement that he leads has sprung from the unwillingness of local Baptist congregations to accept the official leadership of their church. In their view, these leaders have compromised the Church and the faith by collaborating to an unnecessary extent with the government. The leadership has become, in their view, an accomplice of the government and persuades the Church to accept restrictions on its life and worship which deny to it the full practice of the Faith and must eventually stifle it altogether. The strength of feeling against the "betrayers" is evident from the fact that in 1962 the "rebels" excommunicated the whole of the official leadership of the Russian Baptist Church.

Mr. Vins is a representative figure because in every country which is taken over by Communism the same tensions arise in the churches. Is the church to oppose atheistic Communism and, if need be, suffer martyrdom or is it to find some way of co-existing with it? How is the church to survive when the ruling ideology decrees its extinction? This is an agonising decision for all Christians but for the clergy in particular since they are directly responsible for the church and its affairs. Few of them see the issue as clearly or as courageously as Cardinal Mindszenty of Hungary: "When the struggle against the Church began I realised at once that Christianity and Communism were about to measure their strength in a decisive contest . . . our principal task was to hold out where we stood, to alarm Christendom, to call the attention of the whole human race to the danger of Communism."[1] There are not many Cardinal Joseph Mindszentys in any church. Most clergymen, forced to choose between open resistance resulting in dismissal or worse, and some degree of collaboration, choose the latter. They may hope that by so doing they will succeed in winning some concessions for the Church. They may consider that they are of more use to their parishioners at liberty than in a prison camp. But however they rationalise their decision, they are compelled, in order to maintain their position, to make more and more compromises and to see the Church made weaker and weaker by the relentless encroachments of the state.

---

1. Joseph Mindszenty. **Memoirs**, London, 1974. p. 63.

The Minister of Cults nationalises church funds and land, closes church schools, silences church papers and makes church appointments. Anyone who objects will be quickly replaced by someone who doesn't object. In Czechoslovakia, during Dubcek's brief term of office, it was revealed that in the Czech Lutheran Church the whole appointments system, from local level to the highest administrative posts, was tightly controlled by the Communist Party.

There are some who collaborate for honourable reasons: there are some who do so out of fear: and there are some — and church leaders are often amongst them — who do so in pursuit of squalid self-interest. Cardinal Mindszenty in a sermon preached after consecrating a new bishop, said this: "For my part I regarded love of truth as a bishop's most important virtue, which he must not part with out of fear or for praise and advantage; which, in fact, he must cling to even at the peril of his life. The liturgy of consecration also stresses that the bishop may in no circumstances pretend that the light is shadow, the shadow light, or call good bad and bad good".[2] But there are many church leaders who are quite ready to confuse the minds of the faithful at the Party leader's bidding. Appointed to protect the sheep, they readily admit the wolf of Communism into the Christian sheepfold. Revd. Richard Wurmbrand records how "in 1945 a 'Congress of Cults' was held in the Rumanian Parliament building, with 4,000 representatives of the clergy filling the seats. Bishops, priests, pastors, rabbis, mullahs applauded as it was announced that Comrade Stalin (whose vast picture hung on the wall) was patron of the Congress — they preferred not to remember that he was at the same time president of the World Atheists' Organisation . . . One of the chief Orthodox bishops said that in the past many political rivulets had entered the great river of his church — green, blue, tri-coloured — and he welcomed the prospect that a red one should join it, too. One leader after another, Calvinist, Lutheran, the Chief Rabbi, rose in turn to speak. All expressed willingness to co-operate with the Com-

---
2. Ibid.

munists".[3] Rev. Wurmbrand expressed a dissenting view at this Congress and a few days later was arrested: that was the beginning of his 14 years in Communist prisons.

The movement that Mr. Vins leads is inspired by a fervent rejection of the Judases of the official church. This movement co-exists with the official Baptist Church and leaders of Western Baptist Churches have been put in the dilemma of having publicly to choose to support one or the other. Not surprisingly, they have chosen to support their colleagues in the official church. Mr. Vins, to these Western leaders, is an embarrassment. (A leading British Baptist told me that men like Mr. Vins were fanatics and exhibitionists who would only bring reprisals on the whole church). When Dr. Tolbert, president of the Baptist World Alliance, spent seven days in the Soviet Union in 1970, he carefully avoided having any contacts with Mr. Vins' Reform Baptists. A letter signed by Mr. Vins' wife and 12 other Baptists complains of this: "One might have expected that you would have visited at least one of the persecuted churches or would have expressed the desire to meet one of the believers who had recently been imprisoned . . . However, your visit, Brother Tolbert, was to the All-Union Council of Evangelical Christians and Baptists" (the official church) — state shop window for religious freedom ". . . from the height of a royal visit it is of course difficult to notice the tears of the orphans and Christian widows".[4]

A more recent example of how Baptist leaders in the West align themselves with the official Russian Baptist Church occurred in the spring of 1976. The Revd. David Hathaway, who had been imprisoned in 1972 for smuggling Bibles into Czechoslovakia, was organising a petition and protest march in London on behalf of Mr. Vins. 250,000 people signed the petition and long lists of prominent people who supported the protest were published in the national papers. A motion supporting the protest was tabled in the House of Commons. A month before the

---

3. Richard Wurmbrand: **In God's Underground,** London, 1968. p. 27.
4. Quoted by Michael Bourdeaux in an article in the **Times,** 27 April 1971.

march was to take place, Dr. David Russell, general secretary of the Baptist Union of Great Britain and a member of the WCC's Central Committee, returned from a visit to Soviet Russia. He said he had had "frank and open" talks with the leaders of the official Baptist Church and also with the Deputy Chairman of the Council for Religious Affairs, a government official. Dr. Russell had also preached in Mr. Vins' church in Kiev and had expressed sympathy to Mrs. Vins. Dr. Russell would have nothing to do with the protest march which he described as "counter-productive". Revd. Hathaway declared that Dr. Russell had been hoodwinked by the Soviet authorities and that he was naive to accept their assurances. The Anglican **Church Times,** in its leading article on 7 May commented: "Officially, the Baptist Union here has endorsed the views of its general secretary Dr. David Russell, to the effect that only a comparatively small number of Baptists are in prison there and that, thanks to the quiet diplomatic intervention of such as himself with the Soviet authorities, the situation gives little cause for anxiety".

One person Dr. Russell would certainly have met was Mr. Alexei Bychkov, a leader of the official Baptist Church and president of the European Baptist Federation. Mr. Bychkov is also a member of the Russian Baptist delegation to the WCC. When the letter from Fr. Yakunin and Lev Regelson, calling on the WCC to protest against Soviet persecution of Christians, was published at the Nairobi Assembly, an official rebuke from Mr. Bychkov and his colleagues followed! Ignoring all the evidence in the letter of persecution, the official Baptists complained that the activities of the breakaway Baptists had become "the subject of the political game in the West" — an argument familiar enough from Soviet Party propaganda.

Western church leaders who take Dr. Russell's attitude are already collaborating as effectively with the Soviet Government as official church leaders in Russia — yet they lack the excuse of being under physical duress. In their view, there should be no bible smuggling, no protests, no demonstrations. Men like Mr. Vins are inconvenient oddities, best ignored. Everything possible should be done to avoid giving offence to the Soviet government. They believe that the harsher aspects of Soviet tyranny can be mollified by adopting British "parliamentary" methods: patient reasoning, reform of laws and the passing of resolutions in committee. They are concerned with the theory and practice of compromise: how Christians can live harmoniously in a Communist society. In a later chapter we shall consider if this is intended as a psychological preparation for the day when the West itself falls victim to Communism.

Since the first edition of this book was published Mr. Georgi Vins has left Soviet Russia and is now living in the USA. In April 1979 Mr. Vins and four other dissidents were exchanged by the Soviet Union for two top Soviet spies. Mr. Vins' family arrived in the West a few weeks later.

In his first interview with Western journalists, Mr. Vins said :

"Speaking from personal experience, I am convinced that even if I had not been sent out of the Soviet Union I would have been dependent to a large degree on Western support. Whenever there was support action in the West I was treated better by the warders and prison administrators. When there was no support, conditions immediately became worse."[5]

Thus Mr. Vins himself confirms the view taken in these last two chapters; vigorous protest in the West **does** afford some protection to persecuted Christians in Soviet Russia and Eastern Europe. Only the WCC remains unconvinced.

---

5. **Christian World** 4 May, 1979.

Chapter VI

SOVIET JEWS AND THE WCC

IN 1917, there were 3,000 synagogues in Russia. By 1941, there were only 1,011: the rest had been forcibly closed. By 1969, the number had fallen to between 40 and 50. Yet during this period over two million Jews had been added to Russia's Jewish population as a result of her annexation of the Baltic States and the Western Ukraine in 1939!

In 1922, all Jewish high schools and elementary schools were closed. The teaching of Hebrew is now forbidden by law. Except for some small calendars and the Peace Prayerbook of 1956 there have been few Jewish religious publications since 1917. The Peace Prayerbook ran to only 3,000 copies, most of which were sent abroad. In 1962, the baking of matzos — unleavened bread — was forbidden: it is officially regarded as "counter-revolutionary" bread. The ban was raised in some towns after protests from abroad.

It has been estimated that under Stalin and his successors about 1.3 million Jews became the victims of terror campaigns: this was out of a Jewish population of 5.5 million at the time of the Revolution. Not only was Stalin motivated by anti-semitism — when he died he was planning mass drowning of Jews in Lake Baikal — but there is plenty of evidence to support the charge that the Soviet Communist Party has always pursued anti-semitic policies. Since the foundation of the State of Israel, anti-semitism has been concealed under the cloak of anti-Zionism. After the Six Days War in 1967, many Jews were expelled from the Party and the bureaucracy and the number of professions and higher schools of learning from which they were excluded was increased. Reprisals taken against Jews who wanted to emigrate to Israel have been particularly severe: merely to apply for permission to emigrate may result in loss of job and even imprisonment. The attempt — eventually successful — by the ballet dancer Mr. Valery Panov to emigrate to Israel with his wife was one which received wide publicity in the West in 1973. There have been thousands of other attempts that have ended less happily.

Christianity, commonly understood, is the fulfilment of the messianic intention of Judaism. "Spiritually, we Christians are Semites" said Pope Pius XI. Yet in the past the Christian Church has shown little appreciation of that fact. It would, therefore, be ingenuous to expect the WCC to intervene on behalf of persecuted Russian Jews because of their common religious heritage. But had not the WCC committed itself to oppose racism? Was it not concerned to support racial groups "in imminent danger of being physically or culturally exterminated"? Wasn't this why it was making grants to North American Indians and Aborigines and Indian tribes in Colombia? According to the WCC, these ethnic minorities were having to strive to preserve their language, their customs, their culture and their religion against an indifferent and sometimes actively hostile social environment. Are not the Soviet Jews in the same situation? Their ancient language and their religious culture is proscribed and every attempt is made to eradicate their separate identity and Russify them. Are they not entitled to the same measure of compassionate concern as the other groups? Why, the Soviets have even published Nazi-style anti-semitic forgeries for use against the Jews in Socialist countries!

Jews may be entitled to compassion from the WCC but they are not going to get it. This is because the WCC is not concerned with racial oppression in general but only with **white** racism — that is, the oppression of coloured people by white people. And the area where this kind of racism is most offensively obvious is, according to the WCC, South Africa and Rhodesia. The criteria which govern grants of money made by the Programme to Combat

Racism state:

"The situation in Southern Africa is recognised as a priority due to the overt and intensive nature of white racism . . . In the selection of other areas we have taken account of those places where the struggle is most intense and . . . where racial groups are in imminent danger of being culturally or physically exterminated".

In the Sudan in the 1960s half-a-million Christian Africans were massacred by Arabs from the north but the WCC did nothing.

When a WCC official was challenged he replied: "We are concerned with white racism".

In Burundi in 1972, the aristocratic ruling Tutsi tribe put down a rebellion by the Hutus and then practised a sort of selective genocide. Educated Hutus from government offices, banks, schools — even secondary school children — were herded together and shot and thrown in rivers. 10,000 were disposed of in this way. But it aroused no comment from the WCC: black man was killing black man in a racial war. If white men had been on the winning side it would presumably have qualified for the WCC's attention.

An attempt to challenge the WCC's narrowly exclusive concept of racism has been made by Mr. Sydney Chapman, a former MP. As president of a Committee for the Release of Soviet Jews, he wrote to the WCC in March 1973. He cited the WCC's recent decision to express its abhorrence of apartheid by selling its shares in firms dealing with South Africa. Mr. Chapman suggested that the WCC might consider similar action "to demonstrate your feeling against the tyranny practised by the Soviet Government against its Jewish minority and especially against that section of its Jewish minority which has expressed its desire to leave the USSR". A lengthy reply was received from the WCC explaining why it did **not** intend to do anything about Jews in the USSR. Clearly, the WCC did not feel as strongly about Soviet tyranny as Mr. Chapman. The WCC official wrote: "I am interested in your suggestion that our policy vis-a-vis the racist dominated portions of Africa might be equally applicable to the USSR . . . I must say that I do not easily follow this line of argument". If Mr. Chapman did not fully understand the WCC's attitude towards "racist regimes in Southern Africa", a WCC publication was enclosed to enlighten him. The WCC's reply was dated May 1973. In that same month a WCC commission "rejected suggestions to broaden the dis-investment campaign to take in other parts of the world".

The WCC's reply to Mr. Chapman is characteristic: it refuses to admit that Soviet Jews are the victims of anti-semitic policies and treats Mr. Chapman's appeal as a further opportunity for indulging its obsession with South Africa. But unknown to Mr. Chapman, the WCC, six months before he approached them, had written on the subject of Soviet Jews to Metropolitan Nikodim of the Russian Orthodox Church, complaining of the "education tax" imposed on emigrating Jews. This private approach to Nikodim was first made known almost accidentally in an interview in the Anglican **Church Times** 19 January 1973. Bishop Sansbury, who at the time was general secretary of the British Council of Churches, was asked to defend the WCC against the charge of left-wing bias. The interviewer said: "I haven't heard a squeak from the WCC in support of World Jewry who are protesting against the treatment of Soviet Jews . . . the WCC does a lot of pontificating in public about Africa but is strangely silent about Communist oppression".

The Bishop began predictably enough: ". . . if you deliver strong public attacks on the Soviet Union you may not help the Jews . . ." But the interviewer refused to let the Bishop off the hook. The Bishop then disclosed that Dr. Carson Blake, who was then leader of the WCC, "wrote to Metropolitan Nikodim about oppression of Jews because he sent a copy of his letter to all National Councils of Churches". The present writer obtained a copy of Dr. Blake's letter from the BCC and it is here reproduced in full. It is the only hard evidence of a private approach by the WCC to the Soviet authorities that I have yet seen.

It affords us the only chance we have of judging how effective such private approaches are likely to be. If they are as weak and conciliatory as this letter, they are not likely to command attention. Indeed, as far as I am aware, no reply to this letter has ever been received.

The letter is addressed to Metropolitan Nikodim and is dated 6 September 1972.

"Your Eminence,

You may be interested to know that there is a very negative reaction developing in the West in response to the newly announced policy of taxing Jewish intellectuals who wish to emigrate to Israel according to the amount of education they have received in the USSR. The whole world has admired the progress made by the USSR educational system, its expansion and its availability to all Soviet citizens. But this new tax to be imposed on Israeli immigrants makes Westerners believe that the educational advantages of the USSR are now to be used to control its citizens and to deprive them of their human rights. Furthermore, the new policy seems to ignore the contribution made to the state in their first five years of employment.

"Could you let me know what is the reason behind this new law? Certainly the USSR does not need the money. Is it meant to discourage emigration? Why then has the policy of allowing Jews to emigrate to Israel been recently more generous? Any help you could give me towards understanding this new policy would be greatly appreciated".

Sincerely and respectfully yours,
Eugene C. Blake,
General Secretary

Chapter VII

NORTH AMERICAN INDIANS AND THE WCC

IN November 1972, some 200-300 Indians forced their way into the Bureau of Indian Affairs Building in Washington D.C. and stayed there for six days. They were armed with home-made petrol bombs, clubs and lances. Their leaders vowed to fight to the death to prevent the government re-taking the building. Eventually they were persuaded to leave by a gift of 67,000 dollars and a promise that there would be no prosecutions. When they had gone, it was estimated that damage amounted to nearly two million dollars, 700 paintings had been stolen or damaged and irreplaceable Indian artefacts had been wantonly destroyed. There were holes in the walls, the plumbing system had been ripped out; typewriters and office furniture were smashed and documents and files were inches deep on the floors. During the occupation the Indians were allowed to send out truckloads of files and artefacts unhindered. Their leader, Mr. Dennis Banks, boasted, "We have destroyed the BIA. They ain't got nothin' to work with. We had a truck leave every night".

The Indians were members of the American Indian Movement (AIM) which had been founded in 1968 for the purpose of voicing the grievances of Indians living on reservations to the federal government. But it was not until the following year, 1973, that AIM really made the front pages of the world's newspapers. Wounded Knee, in South Dakota, is famous in Indian history: there, in 1890, 300 Sioux Indians were killed by US cavalry. The village is now part of the Oglala Sioux Tribal Reservation. On 27 February, the quiet village was suddenly invaded by 200 armed militants of AIM. They stayed there until early May, declaring a 40 acre area around the village a "sovereign state" and repelling every attempt to shift them. Several US marshals manning roadblocks on the approaches to the village were wounded by gunfire. The entire life of the reservation was brought to a standstill.

The battle of Wounded Knee did nothing to help ordinary Indians, but it was a publicity triumph for AIM. It brought AIM its first grant from the WCC's Programme to Combat Racism. This was followed in 1974, 1975, and 1976 by further grants totalling 51,000 dollars — about £25,000. The money for such grants as these is drawn from a Special Fund and a WCC statute requires that "proceeds of the Fund shall be used to support organisations that combat racism, rather than welfare organisations that alleviate the effects of racism . . ." The WCC, it seems, is not greatly bothered about **what** methods are used to "combat racism": it does not object to the occupation and destruction of government buildings and the seizure of Indian villages by armed forces. Nor are its preliminary investigations of groups to which it makes grants very thorough. Did the WCC, when it made the grants, know that the leaders of AIM have a string of convictions ranging from repeated common drunkenness through assault and battery, forgery, burglary and armed robbery? One leader, Mr. Dennis Banks, has no less than fifteen convictions! Collectively, they had spent so much time in prison that one Indian activist said that AIM "was cooked up in the Minnesota Penitentiary".

Again, any responsible body, before making such a grant, would want to know if those who were to receive it were genuinely representative of the Indian people. AIM is an urban organisation whose leaders and members have no experience of life on the reservations. It has appointed itself spokesman for ordinary Indians, but has, in fact, been repudiated by most of the elected tribal leaders. During the seige of Wounded Knee a press release was issued by Mr. Dick Wilson, tribal chairman of the reservation, in which he rejected AIM and its claim to be representative. He said that less than 15 of the gunmen were members of the Oglala Sioux Tribe. "The small band of hoodlums from all over the country who have taken over the village at gun-point does not represent the Oglala Sioux nation. They do not speak for the Oglala Sioux people . . . None of AIM's leaders was born here and none ever lived here . . . they have come in here with guns in violation of our laws; they have looted homes, closed churches and schools, and I say they should be arrested for breaking the law and prosecuted . . ."

One of AIM's special interests is the education of Indian children — not education in the conventional sense of the three Rs but what a WCC publication calls "political-participation education". So-called "survival schools" are set up on the reservations, (where there are perfectly good schools already), to teach "true" Indian history and to "represent a challenge to the consumer-oriented, technological US education system". AIM's schools are similar to those set up in the Negro ghettoes of American cities by the Black Panthers for political indoctrination. The timid response of the federal government to AIM's violent demonstrations at Washington and at Wounded Knee was matched by its willingness to give a grant of 113,000 dollars to AIM's schools programme. Was it aware that in doing so it was financing an attempt to "radicalise" the Indian community by teaching it the arts of political violence? Like the WCC the US government either gave its money knowingly or it was culpably ignorant.

In 1976, further evidence of the political nature of AIM appeared in a report of the findings of a Senate Internal Security Subcommittee: the report is entitled **Revolutionary Activities Within the United States — The American Indian Movement**. It is largely based on the testimony of a police officer who held top-level posts in AIM while acting as an undercover agent for the FBI from 1973 to 1975. Among the findings of the Senate panel are that "AIM does not speak for the American Indians" but is a "minority movement" with no more than a few thousand followers; that AIM's revolutionary activities have included hiding explosives and illegally purchased arms and eliminating opponents "in the manner of the Mafia"; that some AIM's leaders "openly consider themselves Marxist-Leninist" and have ties with Communist Cuba, Communist China, the IRA, and the Palestine Liberation Organisation; that AIM is also allied with other American subversive groups including the Communist Party, the Trotskyists, the Black Panthers and the Weathermen Underground.

The report comments on the fact that the media have given AIM "generally sympathetic" coverage and that "many hundreds of thousands of dollars worth of support has come from various offices of the Federal Government and from a variety of religious organisations, Catholic and Protestant". The bulk of this money, it says, "has been used to radicalise the Indians, to stage confrontations like the occupation of Wounded Knee and the occupation of the Bureau of Indian Affairs in Washington DC, and to take care of the personal financial needs of the AIM leaders". The report condemns "the supine attitude of government officials" in dealing with AIM's violent demonstrations. Such attitudes have "strengthened AIM enormously" and "undercut the prestige and authority of the tribal chairmen".

It must remain a matter for some surprise that a group such as AIM, whose activities are compounded of criminal violence and political protest, should command the moral and financial support of the Churches. It should be remembered that the ordinary church member can exert no influence over his church leaders in these matters. The WCC grants are made to groups recommended by the national Councils of Churches and the leadership of these Councils is usually sympathetic to radical left-wing politics and, therefore, unrepresentative of the ordinary churchman. During the seige of Wounded Knee, 20 representatives of the US national Council of Churches were ordered by police to leave the reservation: they had been giving legal and material aid to the occupying militants. And as soon as the seige had ended the NCC launched a bail fund for those arrested with a donation of 25,000 dollars.

The published statements of the WCC give no idea of the true nature of the groups that receive grants. African terrorists, according to the WCC, are exclusively occupied in social, educational and humanitarian work and Black Power activists are endowed with the loftiest moral sentiments. At the time of Wounded Knee the Programme to Combat Racism expressed its "solidarity with the entire Indian people in their struggle for recognition of their fundamental rights". The statement went on to condemn the USA's "policy of extermination, ethnocide and exploitation continuously practised in that country. Confrontations like those at Wounded Knee are the inevitable consequence of such a policy. To view Wounded Knee as a military operation is to refuse to recognise that Indians are seeking from the US government the redress of legitimate grievances".[1]

Enough has been said in this chapter to show that such a statement gives a totally mistaken notion of what was happening at Wounded Knee. But what should also be noticed is the highly moral, even self-righteous, tone of the statement. Who would suspect that behind it lay the unpleasant reality of AIM's criminal hooliganism? Any church member, inquiring into such matters as the disposal of church funds, and reading similar statements, would probably conclude that all was as innocent as it seems, That, after all, is what he wants to believe. He is disinclined to believe ill of his own church leaders. Only a few will continue with their questioning and an even smaller number will have the time and mettle for the necessary research. The great majority of ordinary church members will continue to put their trust in their churches. It is that trust which the WCC and the national Councils of Churches exploit.

---

1. WCC Press Release, 21 May 1973.

Chapter VIII

WCC AND THE VIETNAM WAR

THE WCC's opposition to the United States' part in the Vietnam War was a necessary consequence of its general view of world politics. According to this, the North Atlantic powers exploit and oppress the developing countries and keep them in a state of subservient poverty They refuse to recognise the legitimate aspirations of these countries for independent national life free from the strangle-hold of a world trading and monetary order which always works to the poor countries' disadvantage. When such countries try to remedy their situation by revolutionary action, the USA can be expected to intervene with military supplies and, if need be, troops. She will justify her actions by the "containment of Communism" theory. This is merely an attempt to give ideological respectability to a brutal economic imperialism. By appearing to fight Communism, America is able to keep in power in the Third World those corrupt ruling elites that favour her own interests. America benefits commercially and strategically from such a partnership while the ruling elite is assured of American military support against the popular demand for a people's government.

That is a fair summary of the WCC's view of world politics: it could be substantiated from dozens of WCC documents. The absence of any reference to Soviet Communism as a threat to the Western world is very striking. Indeed, the struggle between Communism and the free societies has altogether disappeared, to be replaced by a struggle between poor Third World countries and the rich and wicked North Atlantic powers. Totalitarian Communism is no longer a military and ideological threat to the Free West but is now seen as the bringer of liberty and material blessings to the oppressed and deprived peoples of the Third World. America is also translated: no longer the home of the free, she is now the bogeyman of world politics, operating a global system of ruthless economic imperialism. Dark has become light, and light dark.

Against this background, it is understandable that at its 1966 World Conference on 'Church and Society' the WCC should blame the USA for the Vietnam War. It condemned the "use" of Third World nations as "instruments of Cold War politics" resulting, it said, "in several international wars of major proportions, such as those in Korea and Vietnam, as well as many lesser conflicts".[1] It denounced the USA for supporting oppressive elites in developing countries — presumably because this obstructs the advance of Communism. "The major nuclear powers", it said, "are under obligation not to prevent, through their intervention, the occurrence of the necessary changes..."[2] The WCC then stated that "the massive and growing military presence in Vietnam and the long-continued bombing of villages in the South and of targets a few miles from cities in the North cannot be justified. They involve the danger of escalation of the war into a world conflict and do not bring South Vietnam closer to political stability or solve the problems which have produced a revolutionary situation in that country".[3]

The WCC kept up a constant barrage of criticism of the USA from the earliest days of America's involvement in the war. Only when America finally withdrew her forces, allowing the Communists to overrun the South, did the barrage cease. The WCC threw all its considerable weight behind the international anti-Vietnam peace campaign which, for all its moralising had a political rather than a humanitarian objective: it could only be satisfied by the defeat and humiliation of America. According to this movement's political mythology, America was the

1. **Church and Society**, p. 140: the WCC's official report, 1967.
2. Ibid. p. 147.
3. Ibid. p. 148.

"imperialist aggressor" in Vietnam whereas the Communist North was engaged in a crusade to liberate the South from a corrupt and undemocratic regime. This ignored the fact that Communism in Vietnam was not a genuine people's movement, and that when the Communists took over the North, nearly a million showed their hatred of it by fleeing to the South. Nor was it wanted by the peasants of the South: the Viet Cong terrorists who had infiltrated the South had taught them that the alleged corruptions of President Thieu's government were infinitely preferable to the Utopia of Communism. Revd. Michael Counsell was Anglican Chaplain in Saigon from 1968 to 1971. He learned the language of the people and had a deep understanding of them. He has written :

"I am quite certain that none of the Vietnamese people I spoke to wanted to be ruled by Communists; and not one of the families of my acquaintance hadn't lost a father, son or brother murdered by the Communists. Their method was to try to destroy order and the smooth running of society, so that in the chaos which resulted they might persuade some people to think that even a Communist dictatorship would be preferable to the present mess. Small wonder then that few people were prepared to work for the good of society, as by doing so they made themselves targets. In one year while I was there 365 village headmen were assassinated by Communists. That is, every night of the year, one public-spirited citizen who had been foolish enough to offer his services for the good of the community was dragged out of his bed and murdered in cold blood".[4] In such a passage as that, we are able to glimpse a reality which is constantly obscured in WCC documents by political rhetoric and anti-Americanism.

In 1968, as Russian military might threatened the fragile government of President Dubcek in Czechoslovakia, the WCC held a General Assembly at Uppsala in Sweden. There was, of course, no condemnation of Soviet imperialism. Instead a unilateral request was addressed to the

---

4. Very Revd. Michael Counsell in the British journal **Open Eye**, March 1975.

USA to stop the bombing of **military** targets in North Vietnam. An attempt to link this with a condemnation of the infiltration of the South by Viet Cong terrorists was heavily defeated. Since one of the chief objects of the WCC is to convince the West that Communism is benevolent, it could hardly admit that Communists impose their rule in the way described by Revd. Michael Counsell.

Far more agreeable publicity for the WCC's view of the Communist North was provided in 1973 by the Revd. Graeme Jackson on his return from a 7-day visit to Hanoi. Mr. Jackson was at the time deputy director of a WCC department that distributes vast amounts of aid to developing countries. Hanoi, Mr. Jackson says, "is not a typical Asian city. It is cleaner than most. There are no beggars The children show no signs of malnutrition. There are no shanties on its outskirts — no slums in its centre". And North Vietnam is also an unusual Asian country. "For this is a country where hunger, ignorance, disease and unemployment have been banished". It is also a country where "everyone can read and write". In 25 years illiteracy has been abolished. For sheer lyricism, the last paragraph of Mr. Jackson's report recalls the visits of Dr. Hewlett Johnson, the Red Dean of Canterbury, to Cuba, China and Soviet Russia.

"In the mind of the sceptical Westerner raised on the fear of Communism and a belief in the values of our so-called free Western democracies, the question must arise whether these things have been achieved at the price of personal liberty and the crushing and moulding of the human spirit into one uniform pattern. To debate such questions will no doubt relieve the tedium of many of our leisure hours but the memory of the courtesy and gentleness and pride of the people I met; of the straight-limbed, clean-skinned, clear-eyed children playing on the streets of Hanoi; of a crowd enjoying itself at a circus one evening; of the cheerful, alert men and women I saw in Hanoi and the villages round about, leaves me in no doubt as to the answer I would give to that question".[5]

---
5. WCC's **This Month** dated February 1974.

When Mr. Jackson met Protestant church leaders in Hanoi, they spoke "appreciatively of the WCC's position in support of the struggle of the North Vietnamese people". They also welcomed both the criticisms made by Dr. Eugene Carson Blake, WCC general secretary, of America's alleged bombing of dykes in North Vietnam and also the recent Bangkok Conference's resolution against the bombing.

The WCC's Bangkok Conference on World Mission met in the early part of January 1973; the latter end of that month saw the signing of the Peace Treaty that some mistakenly supposed would end the Vietnam War. A great deal of time was spent at the conference on a resolution entitled 'Salvation Today and Indo-China'. It was less of a resolution than a comprehensive denunciation of the USA. "How can we preach the good news of Salvation Today when on the same day a holocaust of destruction is unleashed" — the US bombing of the north — "which is widely believed by its perpetrators to be a defence of freedom and Christian values? How can we discuss a missionary strategy of the Christian Church in our time when millions of Asians are faced with the brutal power politics of countries some of which are made up predominantly of people who profess Christianity?"

The resolution asked the WCC to request North Vietnam "to make positive efforts to establish a workable peace and to accept an international and ecumenical group of Christian leaders to be with the people in the terrorised areas and to share their fate, as a gesture of solidarity with suffering people and as a means to awaken the consciences" of the communities from which the Christians come. It pleaded with President Nixon "who prays to the same God and professes the same salvation" to stop the war now; halt bombing; call American forces home and remain at the conference table so as to "restore himself to the company of those who struggle to understand salvation in its full Biblical meaning".

The use of the word "salvation" in such passages, without any reference to redemption from sin through Jesus

Christ, suggests that the word has been emptied of its theological meaning and filled with a new political one. "Salvation" for Indo-China may be taken as meaning salvation from American troops and American imperialism. A few days before the Bangkok resolution, in his 1972 Christmas message to the Churches, Dr. Philip Potter the new general secretary of the WCC, had stated quite plainly the new, Marxist use of the word "salvation": "Everywhere there are liberation movements struggling against political, economic, racial, social and male oppression. The word 'liberation' frightens many Christians, especially those who are citizens of countries which one way or another maintain or support the oppression of people. But 'liberation' is a good biblical word, for that is what 'salvation' means".

The Bangkok resolution ended by pledging support to all those who "for conscience sake" oppose America's part in the war by refusing to pay taxes or serve in the army. It asked that army deserters be fully accepted as American citizens "who have served their country well".[6] The WCC's encouragement to young Americans to "dodge the draft" or to desert had begun in 1970 when Revd. Rex Davis, an Anglican minister from Australia, was put in charge of a £90,000 scheme to help American Vietnam deserters who had taken refuge in Canada. Mr. Rex Davis's view was that "total desertion from the military would be splendid". The deserter was admired as a hero of the anti-Vietnam campaign who was entitled to be re-settled in another country at the churches' expense and to finish his highschool education. One whole issue of the WCC's quarterly youth magazine **Risk** was devoted to desertion. The cover had the words 'Just Men Desert' in large type superimposed on a picture of a clergyman whose coat was studded with anti-Vietnam and flower-power badges.[7] Inside we are told that the act of desertion is a rebellion against the "oppressive conditions of man" and the "dehumanized world" of Western society. These "conshies" are not those we were familiar with in the Second World War: they

6. WCC's Ecumenical Press Service, 17 January 1973.
7. **Risk,** a WCC youth quarterly, No. 3, 1970.

have no **moral** objection to war and nowhere in the magazine is there any suggestion of moral outrage at being asked to kill. Their objection is ideological, not moral. They object to fighting in Vietnam because it is a war against Communism. It was for that reason that they obtained the support of the WCC.

In July 1972, Dr. Eugene Carson Blake made a personal appeal to President Nixon to stop the alleged bombing of the maritime and fluvial dykes in North Vietnam. The bombing, he said, was a deliberate attempt to produce a "natural disaster". He continued: "I admit it is difficult to give credibility to such allegations, since the magnitude of the human suffering which major ruptures in these dykes would provoke is almost unthinkable". Difficult as it was, Dr. Blake nevertheless **did** accept the allegations and he accepted them on remarkably flimsy evidence. He was unable to produce anything more substantial than an unnamed "foreign journalist" who, he said, had witnessed American planes bombing the dykes, and "Swedish television films" which "show serious bomb damage done to dykes". The USA, of course, did not admit to any intentional bombing of the dykes.

A month after Dr. Blake's appeal the WCC's Central Committee met in Utrecht and issued a statement saying that it "welcomes and supports the stand taken by the general secretary of the WCC against the bombing of the dykes". It went on to demand that President Nixon stop all bombing in Vietnam and withdraw all American troops not later than the end of 1972; "continued US military presence ... in any form is detrimental to peace in Indo-China". Three months before this condemnation of American bombing, the Communists had launched their spring offensive against the South. In the course of this blitzkrieg, their mortars reduced the towns of An Loc, Quang Tri and much of Kontum to rubble — including their hospitals. As columns of refugees fled from shattered Quang Tri the Communists literally shredded them with Russian made guns and over 20,000 were killed or wounded. Sir Robert Thompson described this as "the most calculated act of butchery during the whole war".[8] Yet the Central Committee made no mention of this or of any other Communist atrocity.

Dr. Blake's condemnation of the USA for the alleged bombing of the dykes found further support in an open letter written by Metropolitan Nikodim of the Russian Orthodox Church to President Nixon. Nikodim, as well as being a member of the WCC's Central Committee is president of the Christian Peace Conference (CPC) and it was in that capacity that he wrote to the President. "In the name of the Gospel of the Lord Jesus Christ, and compelled by our conscience, we turn to you and ask you to put an end to the terrible and unprecedented destruction of human life and total human environment which American forces at your command are carrying out in SE Asia. As human beings and as Christians, we demand that you immediately stop this unspeakably horrible war against the peoples of SE Asia".[9]

No one who is familiar with the brief history of the CPC would expect its president to be anything other than vehemently anti-American. It was founded in 1958 by the Czech theologian Mr. Joseph Hromadka and its headquarters are in Prague. Mr. Hromadka spent the years of the Second World War in the USA studying at Princeton Theological Seminary. At the end of the war, he returned to his native land and since then has lost no opportunity of denigrating the country that once sheltered him. The CPC may be described roughly as the Soviet bloc's attempt to create a parallel body to the West's WCC. Its main purposes are to give Soviet foreign policy the appearance of moral justification and to propagate the idea that Marxism is the necessary social expression of the Christian Gospel.

The CPC is specially important as a seed bed where ideas are germinated for later transplantation to the West. Much of the WCC's political ideology has been received in this way from the CPC. Mr. William Fletcher, the

8. Sir Robert Thompson in an article 'The Human Cost of Communism' in **Daily Telegraph** 7 September 1972.
9. **Church of England Newspaper** 4 August 1972.

American historian, considers that the whole liberal mythology of the Vietnam War, in which the USA was cast as the aggressor in collusion with a corrupt and dictatorial South Vietnamese government, had already been worked out by the CPC before it became fashionable in the West. "The CPC's treatment of the Vietnam conflict," writes Fletcher, "was a constant, long-term, patiently waged, and ultimately, highly successful struggle".[10] By communicating its Soviet view of the Vietnam War to the WCC, and thence to the Western Churches, the CPC played an important part in stirring that great tide of antiwar feeling that eventually undermined America's self-confidence and forced her to surrender.

Metropolitan Nikodim, occupying a commanding position in both the CPC and the WCC, has been a subtle and effective agent in this transfer of ideas. When Nikodim made a public statement on the Vietnam War it was quite impossible to tell whether he was speaking as president of the CPC or as a member of the WCC: both bodies were united in a common denunciation of the USA. Nikodim was able to ensure that an identity of views was achieved by these two bodies, one from the West and the other from the Communist East. Here is Nikodim at the WCC's 1966 'Church and Society' meeting: "When I speak of the needs and problems of the contemporary world, there rises before me the image of the valiant, struggling and suffering people of Vietnam and the heart of man cannot but be filled with sacred indignation before the cruel and unlawful action of the United States in Vietnam".[11] Two years later, he said that "the greatest transgression" against earthly peace "is the aggression of the USA in Vietnam, spawning its cruelty and inhumanity, and truly called a bleeding wound on the body of humanity".[12] The language is perhaps a little too luridly melodramatic for a Westerner but Nikodim's politics are bent in the right direction. In 1975 at the WCC's Nairobi

---

10. William C. Fletcher, **Religion and Soviet Foreign Policy 1945-1970**, p. 47, OUP, 1973.
11. Ibid. p. 122.
12. Ibid.

Assembly he was rewarded for his loyalty to Soviet foreign policy directives by being promoted to one of the WCC's six presidential chairs.

When the Peace Treaty was signed in January 1973, the withdrawal of American troops was in sight. Under the terms of the Treaty all US troops had to be evacuated within 60 days. It was probably the only part of the Treaty that was honoured. The Treaty was never meant to end the war — it was merely a diplomatic device to enable America to get out of Vietnam without losing too much face. Five American presidents had pledged their support to South Vietnam and President Johnson had unequivocally declared, "We will stand in Vietnam". South Vietnam was also entitled to protection by SEATO in a treaty formally signed by the USA. But now America was getting out and she was getting out in a hurry. The Treaty guaranteed the South a one-for-one replacement of weapons but it was a promise that was never kept. The US Congress cut back on military aid for Vietnam and tried to forget that the war had ever happened.

America's will to fight the war had been crippled and she had been made practically ungovernable by the anti-Vietnam peace lobby. To some it was a humiliation and a defeat without parallel in her entire history. But to the WCC and Church leaders throughout the West, the withdrawal of the USA from Vietnam was a moral triumph and the consummation of a decade of tireless propaganda. It was celebrated also by those leftist groups with whom the churches had made a common front.

But the war was not over. When the so-called Peace Treaty was signed, the Communists still had 300,000 troops in the South and the Treaty did not require them to withdraw! Instead they moved another 100,000 down to join them. They also extended an oil pipeline that ran from Communist China, through the demilitarized zone and into the South to feed their 600 tanks and 600 heavy artillery pieces. A year after the signing of the Treaty, 1,000 soldiers a week were still being killed in the South. The North had never had any intention of abandoning its aim of taking the South by force: the Treaty negotiations provided a convenient "breather" enabling it to strengthen its position in the South. In the first days of 1975, the Communists launched their last savage assault upon the South.

Westerners watched on their colour television screens as the great migrations of refugees fled before the Communist attack. There were an estimated two million refugees, destitute, homeless, starving. Village by village was remorselessly shelled into submission. At last Saigon fell, the TV screens were blank and the refugees were trapped between the enemy and the sea. Many thousands set out in tiny overcrowded boats to sail . . . to where? "My withers are not wrung by these South Vietnamese sob-stories" said Mr. Gough Whitlam, Labour Prime Minister of Australia after first consulting with the government of North Vietnam.

Then came reports of the capture of the beautiful Cambodian capital of Phnom Penh — "city of flowering trees and gold-roofed temples". The Communists expelled the whole population of the city — two million people — into the surrounding countryside. They were driven out at gun-point, the young, the old, aged and infirm, even hospital patients were wheeled out in their beds, trailing saline drips, pushed out by their relatives to die in the hills. These scenes were witnessed by Dr. M. Carmichael, an anaesthetist from Edinburgh who was with a medical team in Cambodia. "There were some amazing scenes. The sick really were wheeled away in beds to God knows where — out into the country along what used to be main roads. Goodness knows what happened to them and to the old people".[13]

An estimated one million Cambodians have since been killed by the Communists.

The Western world was shocked by the ferocity of the Communist attack and by the Communists' indifference to the misery of the civilian refugees. It was shocked but strangely silent. And not a single Church leader raised his

---

13. Report in **Daily Telegraph** 9 May 1975.

voice in protest at the carnage. Nothing is more revealing of the true objectives of the WCC than its silence at that time. As long as American troops were fighting in Vietnam, it kept up a constant campaign against the war: when US troops left, the WCC's protests were heard no more. In 1971 an advertisement appeared in the **International Herald-Tribune** headed 'Stop The Killing Now!' It said the war in Vietnam must be stopped "not only for the sake of the Vietnamese and the Laotians and the Cambodians and the young American soldiers, but for all our sakes. Our sense of humanity cannot survive these inhuman indecencies". A number of prominent churchmen appended their names to this advertisement: amongst them were Dr. Blake of the WCC, Lord Soper, Lord MacLeod, Canon John Collins, Dr. Martin Niemoller, Dr. Kenneth Greet, Archbishop Helder Camara. Lords Soper and MacLeod and Dr. Neimoller are well-known pacifists yet neither they nor any other of the signatories was heard to denounce the "inhuman indecencies" of the Communist onslaught on the South in 1975. The agonies of the Vietnamese people were never more severe than when Communist rockets and artillery shells were pounding the towns and villages of the South filled with frightened refugees in the last weeks of the fighting. The subsequent genocide in Cambodia is now well documented. But not a word of protest was uttered by these church leaders. Perhaps their "sense of humanity" was outraged only when non-Communist **Americans were killing?**

Another example of how suddenly the protests ceased once the Americans were withdrawn is afforded by the storm of protests over the US bombing of the North. Just before the Peace Treaty was signed, the WCC denounced the bombing of Hanoi; Pope Paul VI also denounced it and the Archbishop of Canterbury called it a disgrace to civilisation. Cardinal Krol of Philadelphia and other churchmen took part in a silent protest march to the White House and in London Bishop Trevor Huddleston delivered his own personal protest to the American Embassy. The first act of Dr. Philip Potter, who had just replaced Dr. Blake as leader of the WCC, was to write to President Nixon objecting to the bombing. "We have read with horror . . . that during the last days there has been the heaviest bombing yet, with the subsequent killing and maiming of people and the destruction of the Indo-Chinese countryside". These indignant protests were fashionable while America was involved in Vietnam, but consciences were less sensitive to the horrors of war after the Americans had left. Are we to conclude that such protests were motivated less by a Christian abhorrence of war than by anti-Americanism?

For ten years, from 1965 until the war ended in 1975, the WCC poured vast quantities of aid into Indo-China. Nearly ten million dollars worth was apportioned between North and South Vietnam. Some charities — Oxfam for example — confined their help to the South, not because they did not want to help the North, but because the Communists would not allow facilities for seeing that aid was properly used. This did not deter the WCC. In the same way that it gave money to African terrorists without insisting on evidence of how the money was spent, so it gave food, medical supplies, building materials and so on to the North. 750 tons of corrugated iron sheets were delivered on one occasion to the Communists. No doubt there were other materials delivered that could have been useful to the North's war effort. The aid went on during the war and continued after the capture of the South. Even when the Communists were bombarding Saigon in the last weeks of the war, there were reports that the WCC was still sending food to the Viet Cong, or the Provisional Revolutionary Government as it was euphemistically termed.[14] At a time when hundreds of thousands were starving in other parts of the world, the WCC might have found a more humane use for their food than giving it to the armies of an aggressive state.

In 1972, the WCC set up its Fund for Reconstruction and Reconciliation in Indo-China. It budgeted for five

---

14. Reports in **Private Eye** 21 March and 30 May 1975.

million dollars apportioned as follows :
2,000,000 to North Vietnam
2,000,000 to South Vietnam
500,000 to Laos
500,000 to Cambodia

Closer examination of these figures disclosed that half of the sum donated to South Vietnam was, in fact, going directly to the Provisional Revolutionary Government, that is, the Viet Cong, the terrorist arm of the North. The PRG (which has since been abolished) was never anything more substantial than a propaganda myth of the North and it is a measure of the degree to which the WCC had committed itself to the Communist cause that it was prepared to grant a million dollars to it. The international anti-Vietnam lobby made effective use of the PRG myth by treating PRG as if it actually ruled over a definable territory like any other government. In fact, of course, the only territory it held was what it had won by terrorist infiltration of the South, and this territory was still under the legally constituted government of the South. The PRG had no capital, no currency and lacked all the customary attributes of sovereignty. Yet in spite of its obvious deficiencies, the WCC chose to treat PRG as a legitimate government.

The WCC reported on the progress of the Fund in the autumn of 1974. The two million dollars for the North was being spent on the rebuilding and equipping of a hospital at Hai Duong which was alleged to have been destroyed by American bombing. More than half of the money for Laos had been committed to reconstruction work, but Cambodia was not mentioned. Of the million dollars earmarked for South Vietnam only 150,000 dollars had been used: a committee had been set up but it had not yet "led to any programme of action which can be funded". In contrast the whole of the million dollars awarded to the PRG had been spent. In such ways even an aid programme with the innocent-seeming title of "reconstruction and rehabilitation" can be given a political bias.

The WCC's support of the Communist North throughout the Vietnam war raises the question; What of Indo-China today? What has the Leftist anti-war movement achieved by its undermining of American aid to Vietnam? From the infrequent reports that leak from Vietnam and Cambodia there can be no doubt that those unhappy countries are now in the grip of a ruthless Communist terror state. Writing in 1977, Revd. Michael Counsell — from whom we quoted earlier — has this to say: "Khieu Samphan, one of the Cambodian Communist leaders, stated in a recent interview with an Italian magazine that before the war the population of Cambodia was seven million; that one million had died in the war and that the population now is five million. When asked what had happened to the other million, he replied: 'Why are you so concerned with war criminals?'

"So, by the Communists' own admission, something like a sixth of the population have died since they came to power. Reports from refugees indicate that about 100,000 people have been executed by being shot or beaten to death, or run over by bull-dozers 'to save ammunition.' A deliberate policy has been to eliminate the whole of the previous Cambodian army, all those with more than a basic education, all teachers, religious leaders, local officials, and those who criticise the hard-work programme of the new regime. The populations of the towns have been marched into the countryside and chained to ploughs, and those who were too weak were left to die by the roadside. Those who still live are given a ration of eight ounces of rice a day and nothing else, and there are no medicines. 100,000 Cambodian refugees have fled into Thailand. They have walked long distances over the mountains. Some were killed by the landmines along the border. Most were suffering from malaria and had the swollen bellies which indicate prolonged malnutrition."[15]

The WCC, by its persistent propaganda on behalf of the Communists, is partly responsible for the present suffer-

---

15. Very Revd. Michael Counsell in an article: 'The Crucifixion of Cambodia' in **Church Times** 29 April 1977.

ings of the people of Indo-China. Is it the WCC's intention that this same Communist tyranny should be spread throughout the rest of the Third World? That is not a question to which we are likely to get an answer. The WCC's work in Indo-China is completed and it has no interest in what takes place there today. But there is another question, raised by the WCC's support of the Communists during the Vietnam War, to which Westerners should give serious attention. It is a question which raises far-reaching issues of national loyalty and security. Would Britain, in the Second World War, have allowed her churches to denounce British war aims, to encourage members of the armed forces to desert, and to send aid to her enemy? It is, of course, unthinkable. Yet this is what Western — particularly American — churches were doing from 1965 to 1975 by being members of the WCC. It is difficult to see how any country that wishes to survive, can tolerate churches that, in the event of a war, are likely to function as a fifth column.

Chapter IX

SOUTH KOREA: ANOTHER VIETNAM?

DURING the Second World War, Korea was occupied by the Japanese. At the end of the war, the Japanese left and Korea was divided at the 38th parallel, the Soviets occupying the northern territory and the Americans the south. The Soviets rapidly imposed a Communist police state on the North. This was in accordance with Stalin's view expressed to Milovan Djilas: "This war is not as in the past: whoever occupies a territory imposes on it his own social system. Everyone imposes his own system as far as his army has power to do so. It cannot be otherwise".[1]

Two million peasants — one fifth of the North's population — fled to the South to escape the rigours of the new regime. Five years later, in 1950, seven Communist divisions struck at the South without warning. Equipped with Russian T-34 tanks and Yak fighters they crossed the 38th parallel and the Korean War had begun. Later in the war, the Chinese fought as allies of the North. In 1953 an armistice was signed that gave victory to neither side. American casualties were 190,000 and total casualties four million.

With this background, it is not surprising that South Koreans have a very lively fear of Communism and live in constant expectation of another attack from the North. South Korea is even more vulnerable than South Vietnam was. From the border to the southernmost tip of the peninsula is only about 250 miles and Seoul, the capital, is less than 50 miles from the border. Each side has massed about half a million troops at the border and in

---
1. Milovan Djilas, **Conversations with Stalin.** 1963, p. 90.

1975 several tunnels were discovered extending from the northern side of the border under the demilitarized zone. There is evidence of some 14 tunnels. The Communists have been digging these since 1972 and some of them have exits onto the Chorwon Valley considered one of the two main invasion routes from North to South.

The North has also made determined efforts to infiltrate its agents into the South and in 1968 the two regimes came perilously close to war when 31 guerillas from the North attempted to assassinate President Park. (In 1974 another attempt on the President's life failed but his wife was shot and killed). In that same year, 228 Communist agents from the North were killed in the South. In 1972 President Park proclaimed martial law and shortly afterwards introduced a new constitution which enabled him to remain in power indefinitely. Although President Park's own party, the Republican Democrats, has a favoured position in the National Assembly, there is still a vigorous opposition party. In a country that is in a state of seige, it is to be expected that political liberty has suffered some curtailment. There has been a crack-down on subversive and pro-Communist parties but there can be little doubt that in doing so, President Park has the support of the great majority of his countrymen. They are sensible enough to recognise that their country is under continual threat of invasion and that national security must, therefore be given priority.

Such considerations have not deterred the WCC and Western churches generally from denouncing President Park's regime as if it were the most ruthless of tyrannies. In 1973 the WCC printed a so-called **Korean Christian Manifesto.** This was claimed to be a document secretly brought out of Korea though it authorship is not disclosed. In the preamble to the text we are told that the President has brought to South Korea "a degree of police state terrorism and totalitarian control unmatched even during the last corrupt days of Syngman Rhee and rivalled in modern times only by the brutality of the pre-World War Two Japanese colonial period". In the text itself, we are told that the President has "destroyed rule by law and persuasion and has instituted rule by brute force and threat alone . . . the present regime has been suppressing freedom of conscience and freedom of faith. There is neither freedom of speech nor freedom of silence. Worship services, prayer meetings, the content of sermons and prayers and, above all, the teaching of the Bible . . . all have been constantly and unjustly interefered with . . . the present regime . . . in its attempt to control the people, uses systematic deception and manipulation of information, and thorough-going propaganda and brainwashing . . . the mass-media have been spreading half-truths and groundless falsehoods . . . the security networks are used in cruel and ruthless ways, similar to the Nazi's Gestapo and Stalin's KGB . . ." The manifesto ends by urging the people of Korea to withdraw their support from President Park's regime and instead to "build various forms of solidarity among the people to struggle for the restoration of democracy in South Korea".[2]

In October 1974, when a delegation from the churches visited South Korea, they reported feeling "caught up in a climate of fear" that seemed to run right through society so that "many persons were unable to speak freely". One member of the delegation was Dr. Cho, a president of the WCC, who presented to the South Korean Government a statement issued by the WCC's Central Committee protesting at the violations of human rights. In June of the following year, another delegation went to South Korea and reported on its return that national security was "a paramount concern of the fiercely anti-Communist South Korean people". One member of the delegation, Dr. Leopoldo Niilus, director of the WCC's Commission of the Churches on International Affairs, added this: "Security is a perfectly legitimate concern of any self-determining people but we heard many voices saying that a strong, free and democratic nation is ultimately the best security".

---

2. EPS 18 March 1976.

The Korean Government defends itself against the charge of suppressing human rights by claiming that "freedom of religion is guaranteed 100% . . . but we have to take action against those persons who try to undermine political stability through Communist ideology . . . Those Protestant ministers who have been imprisoned have violated the constitution and basic law of this country. That's why they are imprisoned, not because of their religious beliefs".[3] Certainly there is freedom of religion: there are more than 17,000 churches serving the 35 million population and the Christian population is growing four times faster than the birth rate. What of the other part of that government statement? What evidence is there for the government's assertion that they only arrest politically motivated ministers?

Perhaps the most widely publicised case has been that of the signatories of a **Democratic Declaration to Save the Nation.** 18 of these were tried in 1976 and convicted of attempting to instigate a popular rising. They were given prison terms varying from two to eight years. The **Declaration** was first made public at an "ecumenical prayer service" in Myong Dong Roman Catholic Cathedral in Seoul. It demanded that freedom of speech, assembly and publication be "returned to the people", that parliamentary procedures be restored and that the judiciary should once again be independent of the government. The declaration went on to criticise the government's economic policy, in particular its concentration on the export industry as the focus of development. "It was an illusion to achieve a huge modern industrialization upon the ruin of an agricultural economy. The economic system which is dependent on foreign capital contained from the beginning the factor of corruption. If this present state of affairs continues, the breakdown of the economy is only a matter of time. The present regime has lost any capacity to save the nation from bankruptcy . . . the regime

---

3. Quoted in article in **Church of England Newspaper** 2 January 1976.

has no other alternative but to resign".⁴ It is difficult to see what such a document has to do with a service of prayer in a cathedral. Perhaps some explanation is to be found in the mixture of religious and political leaders who were arrested after the service. These included the former president of Korea, the leader of the opposition party, a former foreign minister, a "women's liberation" leader, two professors who had been dismissed from Hankuk Theological Seminary, (one of them was a member of a WCC committee on education and renewal), and several Protestant pastors.

Mr. Martin Bax, Associate Director of Christian Aid, visited South Korea in 1976. He found how fiercely anti-Communist the South Koreans are: "Christians in particular had little sympathy with the North's appalling record in regard to religion. Persecution had been so widespread that there is virtually no church left in North Korea . . . But as strongly practising, believing Christians they know what rampant capitalism has done to South Korea. When they look at the blatant injustices and lack of fairness which have developed over the last 20 years, they can't keep quiet. They feel they have a responsibility to do something about it".⁵ If Christian ministers in South Korea are attacking "rampant capitalism" then it's not at all surprising that plain clothes policemen attend churches to listen to sermons. Nor is it surprising that some of them are arrested — to quote the government's own statement — for trying to "undermine political stability through Communist ideology".

South Korea is a developing country that has wisely preferred capitalism to socialism: with the result that it has been extraordinarily successful. Dr. Colin Clark after recording South Korea's remarkable 8% increase in urban employment, (4% is more usual), continues; "South Korea has not only substantially raised its agricultural productivity, but also produced substantial 'food-substitutes' in the form of manufactured exports. A country which can attain

---
4. EPS 2 August 1973.
5. Interview in **Church of England Newspaper** 5 March 1976.

anything like this rate of growth will soon solve its unemployment problem".[6] It is tempting to suppose that South Korea has incurred the disfavour of the churches by being not only anti-Communist but also a highly successful capitalist country.

Of special interest is the part being played in South Korean church politics by the so-called "industrial mission". Dr. George Ogle was an American Methodist missionary in South Korea who was deported in 1974 for being a political agitator. The case was reported in most Western church papers as if Dr. Ogle was a missionary in the traditional sense of that word — a Bible in one hand and a first aid box in the other. In fact Dr. Ogle was a lecturer in labour-management relations at Seoul National University which closed down shortly after Dr. Ogle left after anti-government student riots. He was the founder of the first Christian industrial mission in Korea.

According to a document published by the WCC — the author "prefers to remain anonymous" — the "first line of opposition" to President Park's government "came from a small group of Christian ministers and laymen engaged in industrial-urban mission. Industrial mission was begun in 1961. Its involvement in labour education, union organisation and labour disputes brought it into frequent conflict with the government . . . In the mid-sixties industrial mission branched off into urban mission and a small number of young ministers began to live among and help organise the large numbers of slum dwellers of Seoul. Again the authorities instead of attempting to secure the co-operation of these young Christians tried to suppress them. There were frequent arrests and constant intimidation". The missions soon linked up with anti-government student groups who in turn made Christian students "sensitive to social and political affairs". The document describes how "the first anti-government action was taken on Easter of 1973. At the sunrise service Christian students circulated an anti-government prayer among the wor-

---

6. Dr. Colin Clark in an article in the journal **Christian Order** July 1975, p. 405.

shippers. Some two months later the instigators of this act were discovered and sentenced to prison terms . . . the leaders were students and young ministers involved in urban mission; and the man held responsible and sent to jail was a pastor of a large Presbyterian Church". The writer adds with evident satisfaction that after that sunrise service "student demonstrations became epidemic. Successive demonstrations were held at Seoul National, Koryo, Yunsei, Ewha, and several other universities. A goodly number of them were under the leadership of Christian groups. Church congregations and church student groups also made a variety of protest demonstrations".[7]

The WCC's Commission on World Mission and Evangelism provides an international advisory service which keeps some 500 urban industrial missions in touch with each other. Apart from Korea, there are UIM's in Argentina, Chile and Thailand and in all these countries the Christian staff "have suffered physical abuse, harassment, imprisonment, loss of jobs and even exile". But we are told by the WCC that this is because they "are taking seriously the Bible's demands for faithful witness to the Gospel among peoples of low economic and social status".[8]

The pattern that clearly emerges in South Korea is that of an alliance between politically motivated Christian leaders and anti-government forces. The WCC understands mission in social and political terms: it tells us that the mission of the Church today is "to participate in the movements of human liberation" not to purvey "some ready-made confessional or theological corpus of Christian truth". If the churches have committed themselves to a political gospel they must not complain when they are charged with political subversion. Their missionaries forfeit the traditional status of the missionary when they abandon the traditional gospel. Nor should church and secular newspapers write about Christians being "persecuted" in South Korea. The Revd. Dwight Malsbary, an American

---
7. WCC's monthly, **This World:** July 1974.
8. **Uppsala to Nairobi,** edited David Johnson, WCC, 1975. p. 87.

missionary there, has complained of reports in the **Washington Post** that the Church in Korea is persecuted. "The churches in Korea are **not** persecuted, the government only arrests disturbers of the peace. It will tolerate nothing that will help bring Korea to Communist slavery and murder".[9]

As long as South Koreans are under threat of Communist invasion they will pay little attention to the politics of Christian "missionaries" who are quite unrepresentative of the Christian community. Mr. Dan Wooding, who visited South Korea at the invitation of a genuine mission society that runs 17 orphanages in Korea, wrote this: "A feature of Korean Christianity is its fiery combination of evangelicalism and anti-Communism, which sometimes amuses Western Christians. I attended a Korean Christian Crusade Preachers' Rally in Seoul. The 300 evangelists are stationed as a spiritual defence line along the demilitarized zone which divides north and south, and also on the islands under threat of a Communist take-over. The earnest preachers told me how they daily take their message out to the people, and how they pray for the day when they can physically trek into North Korea to evangelise their Communist brothers and sisters. The fall of South Vietnam to the Communists has strengthened the anti-Communist resolve of many South Korean Christians, and these preachers laid great emphasis on the teaching of anti-Communism".[10]

Although their activities will achieve nothing more than a nuisance value in South Korea, Christian subversives will be able to marshal what is called "world opinion" in support of their cause. Already a campaign of denigration is being mounted against President Park's regime throughout the Western world. It is a form of psychological warfare which exploits our sensitivity to moral issues in the in-

---

9. In a speech at the International Council of Christian Churches' assembly at Nairobi, 1975. ICCC press release for 16 July 1975.
10. In article 'Fastest Growing Church in World' in **Church of England Newspaper** 2 January 1976.

terests of **political** objectives. It makes a great deal of noise about human rights in South Korea but does not mention the total absence of human rights in North Korea. It demands the restitution of democracy and the release of political prisoners in South Korea but not in the North. Its aim is to weaken Western support for the defence of South Korea by American troops, and to encourage the idea that it would be better for the Korean people if their country were united under one government — that of the Communist North. The success of this campaign will be a signal for the North to attack and there will be another Vietnam in Korea. If that should happen, the churches will bear a very heavy responsibility for the consequent suffering.

Chapter X

MISSIONS AND MARXISM

IN 1971, a group of anthropologists sponsored by the WCC met to discuss the situation of the Indian in Latin America. They published their conclusions under the title **Declaration of Barbados**. The report deplored the impact of Europeans on Indian society; accusing them of the destruction of Indian culture; theft of Indian property and the appropriation of land, labour and natural resources. Reviewing Christian missions in Latin America, it said: "We conclude that the suspension of all missionary activities is the most appropriate policy on behalf of both Indian society as well as the moral integrity of the churches involved". An Anglican bishop in Latin America rightly commented, "The tone and language of the document suggest that it comes from a radical group unsympathetic toward Christian mission and lacks a balanced outlook . . ."[1]

The **Declaration** was one of the first public signs that the WCC was preparing an attack on the traditional notions of Christian mission and evangelism. It was not until the last days of 1972, at its Bangkok Conference, that the big guns were fired. The conference was organised by the WCC's Commission on World Mission and Evangelism (CWME) and its theme was 'Salvation Today'.

As previously explained, the WCC regards "salvation" as meaning "liberation" and so clearly it must enforce changes in our previous idea of mission. The goal of the Christian mission has traditionally been the conversion of

---

1. Rt. Revd. Kenneth Howell, Bishop of Chile, Bolivia and Peru in a letter to **Church of England Newspaper** 2 July 1971.

the heathen. But sending missionaries to foreign lands to preach the gospel of Christ is an embarrassment to ecumenical Christianity. In his speech to the conference, Dr. Potter said: "The whole missionary movement now has a controversial character and the CWME is in the middle of it . . . religious liberty now demands not confrontation but dialogue between men of different faiths and ideologies . . . mission and evangelism cannot be carried out by purveying some ready-made confessional or theological corpus of Christian truth . . ."[2] And in his speech, Mr. M. M. Thomas, chairman of the WCC, called even more plainly for the abandonment of traditional Christian mission: "We are living at a time when we are deeply conscious of pluralism in the world — pluralism of human situations and needs, of varied religions and secular cultures, with different traditions of metaphysics, ideologies and world-views, in terms of which Christians themselves seek to express their commitment to, and confession of, Christ. So much so that any kind of a unity in the doctrine of Christ or of Salvation in Christ, which has been the goal of traditional Christian Churches, is to my mind impossible to conceive except in religious imperialistic terms".[3]

So the idea of "pluralism" relativises all religions and ideologies. Regarded with the tolerant eye of the anthropologist they are all merely expressions of different cultures and different social needs and there can be no good reason for preferring one to another.

As well as the "religious imperialism" which, according to Mr. Thomas, vitiates Western mission, there is also economic imperialism. In view of the WCC, the old-style Western mission is rejected in Asia, Africa and Latin America because it is regarded as the spiritual arm of predatory Western capitalism. The Western churches are fatally compromised in the eyes of the developing peoples by being involved in a wicked capitalist system that fattens itself at their expense. (More than half the delegates at Bangkok were from Third World countries). When Dr.

---
2. WCC's EPS This Month, January 1973 pp. 6-9.
3. Ibid, pp. 3-5.

Potter talks about "liberating" people from social and economic oppression, he is not referring only to people in the developing countries: he also means us in the West. After speaking of the "captivity of the churches and missionary agencies to the political, economic, racial and cultural institutions of society" he went on to say that the church "which would be the bearer of salvation today needs itself to be saved, liberated from all that is false to the revolutionary, convicting and renewing nature of the Gospel".[4] And Dr. Potter's words were echoed by the Bangkok Conference itself, when it declared: "Without the salvation of the churches from their captivity in the interests of dominating classes, races and nations, there can be no saving church. Without liberation of the churches and Christians from their complicity with structural injustice and violence, there can be no liberating church for mankind".[5] By "structural injustice" the WCC means capitalist society and the class system. Our eternal salvation is thus made dependent upon our liberation from them.

The immediate task for Christians, therefore, is to achieve political liberation for themselves and for others. In the past, the Christian mission liberated men from captivity to idols of wood and stone. Today the mission must liberate men from the captivity of political and economic systems, in particular, the monopoly of power, money and trade exercised by the Western nations. "Herein lies the mission of the Church", says Mr. Thomas, "it is to participate in the movements of human liberation in our time . . ." It was, perhaps, in an effort to epitomise the two major themes of the Conference — those of religious pluralism and political activism — that Emilio Castro, director of CWME, said: "The affirmation of African culture, the conveying of Indian spirituality and the challenge to social revolution are the starting points for a new day in world mission".[6]

---
4. See 2 above.
5. Ibid. p. 11.
6. EPS 17 January 1973, p. 2.

By any reckoning, that is a remarkable programme for churches and missions that still profess to be Christian.

The Bangkok Conference was a call to liberate the developing countries from both the religious imperialism of the Christian mission and the economic imperialism of American capitalism. The obvious course of action was to shut down the missions and encourage violent revolution. And this was what Bangkok proposed. It recommended a moratorium on the sending of funds and missionaries to overseas missions and pointed out, helpfully, that churches that did this would then be free to "give financial support to those struggling for freedom from unjust and dehumanizing systems perpetuated by dominant nations and bodies" — which is the WCC's usual way of referring to African terrorists. The politicisation of the churches is surely complete when arguments can be found for supporting terrorists rather than missionaries.

The effect of the Bangkok Conference on Western missions was immediate and profoundly disruptive. Within a month of it ending, two of the largest mission societies in Great Britain, the United Society for the Propagation of the Gospel (USPG) and the Church Missionary Society (CMS), had met and decided that, "In the light of the changed relationships between both Churches and nations, summarised by Dr. Emilio Castro at the recent Bangkok Conference . . . the immediate co-operation between the two Societies be in terms of a joint examination and subsequent response to the demands of the current situation and the manner in which it appears to be changing".[7] Two months later, Revd. John Taylor, general secretary of the CMS, (he is now Bishop of Winchester), wrote an article in his Society's newsletter entitled 'Bangkok and After' in which he tells CMS supporters that "mission in the modern world has to include the liberation of oppressed and underprivileged people". To serve this new goal there will be a "policy of careful selection and orientation of missionaries" who will be given a "renewed understanding of the Bible from the point of view of the community of

---

7. **Church of England Newspaper** 16 February 1973.

the oppressed". Mission agencies overseas must "seek consciously to undermine oppression and foster liberation". Churches must "focus their action for development on the poorest people of any society". The aim of education must be "empowering the powerless, giving a voice to the voiceless . . ." Canon Taylor concedes that there are drawbacks to having political revolution as the objective of a Christian mission: "It will be difficult to get this across, both theologically and politically, to the largely middle-class supporters of missionary societies".[8] But the loss of some of its more affluent supporters would not deter CMS from achieving a radical new look. Canon Taylor was confident that Bangkok was pointing in the right direction.

Nor was he alone. Within two years of Bangkok, every major mission society had accepted the WCC's new ideology of mission. Now it was admitted that saving souls, healing the sick, feeding the hungry and educating the illiterate was not enough. Merely to alleviate human suffering was inadequate: we must become revolutionaries and attack the political and economic causes of suffering. Canon Kingsnorth of the USPG wrote that social relief in the Third World should go deeper than educational, medical and agricultural work; it should aim "at changing structures, institutions, and laws of society — in some circumstances it may be revolutionary".[9] After Bangkok, a missionary would find a commentary on Marx more relevant to his work than a commentary on the Bible. Perhaps Dr. Emilio Castro had something like that in mind when he summed up the results of the Bangkok Conference in those enigmatic words — "We are at the end of a missionary era and at the beginning of world mission".

---

8. The quotations are from the April 1973 **CMS Newsletter**, No. 370.
9. Canon Kingsnorth in USPG's monthly paper **Network**, June 1973, p. 2.

Chapter XI

WCC AND THE THEOLOGY OF ANTI-CHRIST

"WE must be careful that we do not give the impression that the Church is an agency for supporting Left-wing politics". That was said by Archbishop of Canterbury, William Temple, who died in 1944. It cannot be said that anyone, least of all Temple himself, paid much heed to the warning.

Archbishop Temple was one of the chief architects of the World Council of Churches. His book, **Christianity and the Social Order,** published during the last war, was largely responsible for swinging the post-war churches decisively toward Socialist thinking. In 1942, Temple, who was then Archbishop of York, presided over the Malvern Conference, attended by 15 bishops and 400 clergymen and laymen. One of its conclusions was that "the Church can point to those features of our existing society which . . . are contrary to divine justice, and act as stumbling blocks, making it harder for men to live Christian lives. In our present situation we believe that the maintenance of that part of the structure of our society by which the ultimate ownership of the principal industrial resources of the community can be vested in the hands of private owners may be such a stumbling block".[1]

Archbishop Temple wanted the more determined "is" substituted for "may be" but was persuaded to give way. In 1945 when the Labour Party won its first post-war victory, Mr. Hannen Swaffer, the Socialist journalist, remarked that it was mainly due to the influence of William Temple.

---

1. R. P. Flindall, **The Church of England, 1815-1948**, SPCK 1972, p. 429.

Opposition to Temple and his advocacy of the proposed WCC came from Dr. Headlam, who was Bishop of Gloucester and had a reputation as an ecumenical theologian. Bishop Headlam could foresee that the WCC, like its predecessor the ecumenical "Life and Work" movement, would be "continually involved in political matters and controversy, and largely influenced by the passion for identifying Christianity with Socialism".[2] Replying, Temple said that when Church leaders met in any future World Council "they will make known their minds on subjects which they debate . . . I hope that those dealing with any controversial issue, and anything political, will be extremely rare, and that the main topic will be . . . evangelism".[3]

The later history of the WCC justifies Headlam's misgivings and shows how deeply mistaken Temple was. In bondage to Leftist politics, the WCC regards evangelism as irrelevant in a world whose most urgent need is social and political change.

Nor is it only evangelism which the WCC has abandoned since Temple's day. In his enthronement address at Canterbury in 1942, Temple spoke of the ecumenical movement as "the great new fact of our era". 35 years later, Temple would have difficulty in recognising the ecumenism in which he believed. In his day, it meant the attempt to unite the divergent traditions of the Christian Churches and it is still popularly understood as that. But concepts can be twisted and hi-jacked, and since Temple, the ideologues of the WCC have been at work on the idea of ecumenism. They have restored to the Greek word "oikumene" its original secular meaning, "all the inhabitants of the earth". The effect of this is that the world "ecumenical" now refers not merely to all **Christians** but to men of all faiths and none at all. One WCC document declares: "We recognise the importance of co-operating at every level with the Roman Catholic Church, with other non-member churches, with non-church organisations,

---

2. Ibid p. 460.
3. Ibid. p. 463.

adherents of other religions, men of no religion, indeed with men of goodwill everywhere".[4]

This universalising of the meaning of ecumenism has enabled the WCC to break free from the constraints of a specifically Christian identity and advance into a strange no-man's-land, a region of relativity where all faiths, ideologies and cultures are equal and where the uniqueness of Christ's revelation vanishes. Here, the ecumenical goal is no longer limited to uniting the churches — it is the more grandiose one of unifying all mankind. This is not a region where most Christians are disposed to follow, but they are unaware that they are the victims of a semantic deception. Ordinary people expect the meaning of words to be unchanging: their trust in words is a reflection of their trust in the person who uses them. But the WCC is constantly secularising and politicising the meaning of words that are familiar to most people only in a theological context. The savants of the WCC agree with Humpty Dumpty: "When I use a word it means just what I choose it to mean — neither more nor less".

With disarming frankness the WCC has styled this new concept of ecumenism "secular ecumenism". In case it might be thought that **secular** ecumenism is less Christian than the old ecumenism, Mr. Robert McAfee Brown, an American theologian who was one of the chief speakers at the WCC's Nairobi Assembly, tells us that it is "the very heart of what the gospel is all about".[5] It is, he says, an invitation to Christians, "to accept the implications of concern for the secular order". And Dr. Potter, after explaining the secularising of the ecumenical movement, says, "That is why the WCC, as an expression of this movement, has become increasingly and concretely involved in the issues which most burningly concern human beings today, like the development of all peoples and of the whole man and woman, the combat against racism,

---

4. Report of WCC's 1968 Uppsala Assembly.
5. Robert McAfee Brown in an article 'Secular Ecumenism: the direction of the Future' in **World Year Book of Religion,** Vol. 2, 1970.

human rights, violence and non-violence in the struggle for justice, to name only a few".[6] But it is noticeable that the "issues which most burningly concern" the WCC do not include the salvation of mankind by the preaching of the gospel of Jesus Christ. For it is not only ecumenism which Mr. McAfee Brown and his fellow theologians have secularised, but also the gospel. What was once believed to contain the promise of eternal salvation still has a use — but only as one of many agencies in the movement for worldwide human solidarity.

Secular ecumenism is an attempt to accommodate Christian mission to the contemporary world: as such it is self-destructive. In the face of religious plurality, it abandons the uniqueness of the gospel and in the face of secularism, it abandons the gospel itself. Is this the intention of the WCC? Does it believe that the Church should "disappear" into secular life; achieve a kind of spiritual anonymity in service to the world and by so doing purge itself of theological arrogance and cultural and imperialistic associations? In the following passage from a WCC document, the WCC's preference for a secular society in which man has "freed himself from magical, religious or ideological views of the world", over a religious society, is barely concealed :

"Secularisation is a process whereby man becomes freed from the presuppositions of metaphysical and religious ideology and attempts to understand and live in the various realms of the world on their own terms. In contrast with the society in which a particular religious ideology sets limits to a genuine search for truth, the secular society not only permits the diversity of religious ideas but also encourages the pursuit of a sincere and open understanding of the factual reality of the universe . . . In the secular society, therefore, man's choices are no longer obligatory and prescribed. Each man is free to seek

---

6. Dr. Potter in his Alex Wood lecture to the Fellowship of Reconciliation in London, February 1974.

his own faith and make his own assumptions about the purpose of being".[7]

Clearly, such a society, in which all religious faiths are relativised, is more suited to the WCC's goal of a unified humanity than a society in which one religion or church is predominant. But does it not involve the WCC in abandoning the uniqueness of the Christian faith?

Did God make a unique and direct revelation of Himself to mankind in Jesus Christ?

Was St. Luke mistaken when he told us, "Neither is there salvation in any other: for there is none other name under heaven given among men, whereby we must be saved" (Acts 4. 12.)?

Are we entitled to render innocuous Jesus's words. "I am the way, the truth and the life, no man cometh to the Father but by me" (St. John's Gospel 14. 6)?

The victory of Christianity in the Ancient World was due to the fact that it rejected all other gods and declared the absolute uniqueness of Christianity. Today, in an age which is seeing the de-Christianising of Western societies, the WCC appears to have united with the forces of modern atheism in demanding that Christianity renounces all its historic claims and embraces a voluntary anonymity.

There is a remarkable passage in one of the Section Reports from the WCC's Nairobi Assembly: headed 'Seeking Community — the common search of people of various faiths, cultures and ideologies', it states:

"We cannot allow our faith, the gift of our sense of community in Jesus Christ, to add to the tensions and suspicions and hatreds that threaten to tear apart the one family of humanity".

The meaning of this is plain: historic Christianity is now an obstacle to a unified humanity. If it wishes to survive it must abandon any claim to uniqueness, and take its place on an equal footing with all other religions and ideologies. This is, of course, an invitation to the Churches to commit suicide but the WCC, with its customary skilful

---

7. Official Report on WCC's **Conference on Church and Society**, WCC, 1967, p. 158.

manipulation of concepts, manages to present it as a salutary exercise in humility.

The unification of mankind is the goal not only of the WCC's religious ideology but also of its political theory. Just as the secular society is believed to free man from the cramping restrictions of an exclusive religion, so must men be liberated, in their political lives, from the narrow confines of class, from attachment to the nation and from their subjection to the selfish economic order of capitalism. This pattern of thought is evident in this extract from a speech by Miss Pauline Webb, Vice-Moderator of the WCC's Central Committee:

"We must see the Kingdom at work in the 'signs of the times'. The present international economic crisis is calling the nations to reassess the injustice of the present economic order and the reckless squandering of the world's natural resources. . . . A massive worldwide act of repentance, in the fullest meaning of that word, in the rethinking of the whole structure of the economic order, is needed if there is to be a sustainable future for the whole of mankind. The world needs desperately to see, as a sign of the Kingdom, a new kind of community. Within the global village of the world, the divisions and isolations have become more terrifying than ever before".

After saying that every Church tradition and every local church was in danger of a false self-sufficiency, she declared our need "to develop a kind of counter-consciousness . . . We need an awareness that our particular experience of Christian community is fragmentary and partial. We need the enrichment of every possible ecumenical, inter-racial and cross-cultural encounter. We need beyond that to identify more fully and with deeper commitment with the struggles of all those who are seeking to abolish the boundaries of race, sex, class, cultural differences and denominational divisions".[8]

---

8. At a conference in London on 'Christian Mission and Evangelisation', reported in **Church of England Newspaper,** 11 February 1977.

Those who invite us to abolish all boundaries in the interest of a "new kind of community" must have in mind the establishment of a classless, egalitarian world state. Such a world state would control not only the "economic order" which Miss Webb is so anxious to "rethink" but also men's minds. For if a unified humanity can be achieved only by abolishing all divisions between men, then the revival of those divisions would be regarded by a world state as a threat to its continuance. A world state that assumed the task of ensuring that no "divisive" ideologies appeared would be quick to denounce them as "revisionist" "fascist" and "against the will of the people". And those who promoted such heresies would be labelled "dissidents". We are entitled, I think, to see in the WCC's new community of a unified humanity, the lineaments of the totalitarian super-state.

In the ideology of the WCC this "one-worldism" combines with Marxism to make a common appeal to mankind: put off, it says, your parochial loyalties to church, religion and nation and recognise all men as your brothers. Wars and bitterness will cease, we are told, when the artificial barriers of class and belief are thrown down and men seek together for peace. Both Marxism and secular ecumenism propose the same triumphant end to human history: by dissolving all differences of belief and allegiance, a global society will come about dedicated to the needs of common humanity.

Marxism is the **political** tool which will enable the WCC to achieve its ecumenical purpose. Marxism is remarkably well-suited to this use since it is not merely an economic theory but has theological undertones that harmonise agreeably with the WCC's ideology. Marx learned his atheism from the German philosopher Ludwig Feuerbach who, in his book **The Essence of Christianity,** used the device of "alienation" to explain Christianity. According to Feuerbach, man projects the unrealised potentialities of his own human nature and worships them as God. Man will "come of age" when he acknowledges that he has created an illusion; recovers his alienated essence, and sets about realising his own potentialities. In this programme for human enlightenment, religion is merely an instrument of man's education, to be discarded when the lesson has been learnt. What is the lesson? Marx himself wrote: "The highest being for man is man himself".

Marx applied the theory of alienation more widely to capitalism and the class society: overthrow capitalism and you will liberate the frustrated resources, not only of production, but also of human nature. Marxism is **messianic** since it claims to liberate man from all that prevents him from achieving that final state of earthly blessedness which is Communism.

But Marxism is also resolutely atheistic and it knows no other "Kingdom of God" than that which can be realised on earth by man's own efforts. By stressing the messianic pretensions of Marxism, some Marxist philosophers like Ernst Bloch have managed to give it a quasi-religious character. In this way they have approached agreement with theologians of the "God is dead" school of theology. The teaching common to both is that man must emancipate himself from his position as a dependent creature by denying God. The serpent's instigation, "Ye shall be like God", is to be understood as the first promise made to man. According to Bloch, this promise was fulfilled by Jesus: "He who sees me sees the Father". Thus Christ becomes the symbol of emancipated mankind, the first Man become God.

The liberation of man from the "God-idea", says Bloch, is the secret theme of the Bible: the liberation of man from capitalism is the aim of Marxism. Inspired by Bloch — both are professors at Tubingen University — Juergen Moltmann constructed his Christian "theology of hope" which has had a deep influence on the ideology of the WCC. Moltmann explicitly calls for a "political theology" — a call answered by the latest generation of theologians from Latin America whose school of "revolutionary theology" insist that Marxism is the unavoidable political expression of Christianity.

Jose Miquez Bonino is typical of this school; his writings have been widely publicised in the West and it is not at all surprising that he now occupies one of the WCC's six presidential chairs. He repudiates the political and theological past, accusing traditional theology of "bending" the Gospel to suit the prejudices of the rich, white world. The "obvious political motifs and undertones in the life of Jesus" have, he claims, remained hidden "until quite recently". He suggests that a politically "engaged" Christian might understand the Resûrrection as "the death of the monopolies, the liberation from hunger or a solidary form of ownership".

It goes without saying that Bonino is anti-capitalist and anti-American and considers that every Christian has a duty to be so. He tells us that if mankind is to be saved from "the blind forces of destruction, waste, exploitation and oppression unleashed by the capitalist system", a world revolution is necessary. Bonino's Marxism is naive in the extreme: in Cuba he sees the "creation of a new man, a solidary human being who places the common good before his own individual interest". Elsewhere in the world he admits that Marxist revolutions have "shown certain disquieting features in relation to personal freedom . . . in joining a movement such as this, the Christian cannot but feel that he is helping to bring about conditions which are not entirely satisfactory"[9]: an exquisite understatement.

The political crudities of such propagandist writing are obvious: what is not so obvious is the transformation of theology that lies behind it. In the writings of men such as Bonino, messianic Marxism has replaced traditional Christian theology. Dr. Peter Beyerhaus, speaking of the WCC's "political theology", has said that it is "in its deepest analysis, a camouflaged atheistic humanism, in which the names of God and Christ are simply cyphers for the real nature and destiny of man. . ."[10]

9. Jose Miguez Bonino, **Christians and Marxists**, London, 1976.
10. Dr. Beyerhaus is Director of the Institute of Missiology and Ecumenical Theology at Tubingen University: reported in **Church of England Newspaper** 9 June 1972.

For some Christians this fraudulent theology is sufficient proof that the WCC is Anti-Christ since it fulfills St. Paul's prediction (2 Thess. 2:11) that even the believers shall believe a lie. There is also an ancient Christian tradition that Anti-Christ will appear as a benefactor of the human race and Vladimir Soloviev described Anti-Christ as "above all others a compassionate friend of man".

Canon Albert duBois, an American Episcopalian, has no doubts: after describing the WCC's "false efforts to unify Christians on a humanistic, man-centred programme", he called upon his congregation to choose now "between the revealed God of history and the Anti-Christ of the WCC".[11]

If the Christian Church is to survive into the 21st century, it will be necessary for all Christians to make that choice.

---

11. Canon Albert duBois, Professor of Church History and Homiletics at Episcopal Seminary, Lexington, USA: in sermon on 9 June 1974.

Chapter XII

ZIMBABWE: A FAILED UTOPIA

"TO us has been given the privilege of being the first Western nation in the last two decades to have the determination and fortitude to say, 'so far and no further' ..."

Those were the words of Mr Ian Smith when he declared Rhodesia's independence in November 1965. Black African nations that had won their independence might slide down through corruption and tribal dissension into chaos but Rhodesia was different: Rhodesians, said Mr Smith, had "struck a blow for the preservation of justice, civilisation and Christianity".

But Mr Smith had reckoned without the shifty diplomacy of Henry Kissinger, American Secretary of State, and John Vorster, South Africa's prime minister, neither of whom shared Smith's stubborn determination to go on fighting the terrorists until they were beaten. Under their combined pressure Smith eventually conceded the principle of majority rule. In 1979 a general election was held in which 70% of the votes went to the black moderate Bishop Muzorewa who consequently became prime minister. This did not please Jimmy Carter, president of the USA, who said the election was invalid as the Patriotic Front terrorists had not been able to field candidates. This view was shared by the "front-line" African states, Zambia, Tanzania and Mozambique, the United Nations and the World Council of Churches.

To meet this objection a conference was held at Lancaster House in London to which the leaders of the Patriotic Front, Mugabe and Nkomo, were invited: their attendance was partly financed by the WCC. Lord Carrington, British Foreign Secretary, presided. It was agreed that Muzorewa should stand down so that another election could be held with Mugabe and Nkomo taking part. A cease-fire was agreed and in 1980 the terrorists came in from the bush. The election was marred by widespread intimidation by all parties but principally by Mugabe's armed terrorists. "The most potent feature of the election campaign"[1] according to one

---

1. p.328 "The First Dance of Freedom", Martin Meredith (1984)

experienced observer was Mugabe's threat to resume the bush war if the blacks did not vote for him. Another wrote: "This was not the triumph of the ballot over the bullet, as Mrs Thatcher claimed, but of the bullet over the ballot".[2] Both Ian Smith and Muzorewa advised postponing the election but could not persuade the Governor, Lord Soames. (No doubt Soames knew what was cooking and had no intention of interfering with the chef). The result was a humiliating defeat for Muzorewa, only 24% of the votes for Nkomo, and 63% for Mugabe who became Zimbabwe's new prime minister. On being elected he cordially thanked the WCC for its "commitment to the principles for which you and we have struggled together".[3]

A jealous rivalry which had always existed between Mugabe and Nkomo now flared up again. Mugabe accused Nkomo of conspiring against him, dismissed him from government office and imprisoned him. There was nothing unusual about this; opposition party leaders in most black African democracies sooner or later end up in prison. But the roots of the rivalry lay deeper than politics. Nkomo's support came from the Matabele tribe whereas Mugabe's came from the more numerous Shona people. Tribal strife is the bane of black African politics and Mugabe moved with characteristic ruthlessness to crush it. He drafted into Matabeleland his 5th Brigade, specially trained in the arts of counter-insurgency in communist North Korea. It was ordered to terrorise the Matabeles into submission. All journalists were banned from the area, a dawn to dusk curfew was imposed and all food stores were closed to prevent the sale of food to the "dissidents". This last was the cause of special hardship to the people who were already suffering food-shortages due to prolonged drought. The Guardian's reporter who was deported from the country estimated that there were 10,000 soldiers in the area. Donald Trelford, editor of the Observer, made a secret night-flight into Matabeleland and brought back a chilling first-hand account. In their 1983 Easter Pastoral Letter the Roman Catholic bishops in Zimbabwe drew the government's attention to "the reign of terror caused by wanton killings, woundings, beatings, burnings and reprisals". But Mugabe contemptuously dismissed the bishops' appeal and the

---

2. "The Long Fields: Zimbabwe Since Independence", William Spring (1986).
3. Ecumenical Press Service, March 27th 1980.

killings went on. The WCC made some deliberately vague remarks: it was not to be expected that it would condemn the man in whom its hopes for a new Zimbabwe were vested. Better to ignore what was going on. That was no doubt also the view of British Foreign Secretary, Francis Pym, who was overheard mumbling—"Mr Mugabe has got to deal with the situation as he finds it and that is what he is trying to do".

A few weeks before Christmas 1985 the WCC held a meeting of church leaders in Zimbabwe; the purpose of the meeting was to devise ways of intensifying opposition to South Africa. Just before that meeting was held Amnesty International published a report on torture in Zimbabwe claiming that "arrests and torture of suspected Government opponents have increased sharply in Zimbabwe." Arrests were made by an Internal Security force believed to be directly responsible to the Minister of Home Affairs. Those arrested and held without charge included MPs, city officials and employees. The report said that since July, 150 such people had been arrested in the Bulawayo area alone. They were denied access to family and lawyers and their whereabouts was unknown. Tortures commonly used on such detainees included beating on the soles of the feet, electric shocks and immersion in water. Prisoners at Stops Camp, Bulawayo, were kept in "cages" open to all weathers. Prisoners could be held indefinitely under emergency powers without being tried. Cases often rested on no other evidence than forced confessions. Acquittals usually resulted in immediate rearrest.

These injustices were not mentioned at the WCC meeting. Was it that the delegates had not had time to read Amnesty's report? Or were they silent out of a delicate concern for the feelings of their host, Mr Mugabe? No, their indifference was not conditional on this circumstance or that: it was *absolute*. Their indifference to injustice in Zimbabwe was the same as their indifference to injustice in Kaunda's Zambia or Nyerere's Tanzania or any other black dictatorship where democracy was a useful fiction. They were simply not interested. There was a time when they were concerned with black people's rights but that was when those countries were ruled by white men. Once the power of the whites was broken the WCC lost interest. Its ruling obsession is with white power and the injustice that flows from the system. Other injustice it simply doesn't see. For this reason the WCC is the most racist of bodies: it only sees injustice when it puts on its racist spectacles.

The extinction of white power in Rhodesia meant that the WCC could concentrate its energies on preparations for the last great struggle against South Africa. Mugabe had barely had time to exchange his battle-dress for a neat prime minister's suit when the WCC issued a revealing statement that began: "Zimbabwe's independence has drastically changed the balance of power throughout Southern Africa. The change has resulted in further strengthening of the struggle both within and outside South Africa against the apartheid regime. It is highlighted by the increasing number of strikes, school boycotts and bomb attacks on strategic targets (eg Sasol oil refineries)".[4] With a schoolboy's delight in destruction the WCC turns its back on Zimbabwe's internal difficulties: boycotts and bombs are more to its taste. In doing so it ignores the advice of one of its own official reports on violence and revolution: "It may very well be that the use of violent methods is the only recourse. But Christians should think of the day after the revolution, when justice must be established by clear minds and in good conscience".[5]

Does the WCC ever reflect on the revolutions it has helped to bring about? Perhaps it is wise not to—it avoids disappointment.

"Whither is fled the visionary gleam,
Where is it now, the glory and the dream?"

Zimbabwe's constitution, drafted by the British, provided for a Westminster-style parliamentary democracy: what Mugabe runs today is effectually a one-party state. The Bill of Rights, embodied in the constitution, is appealed to in vain by those who are wrongfully-imprisoned. The police and the courts are subject to political interference and there is no political opposition that cannot be silenced once it becomes effective. In Ian Smith's day the Rhodesian Front controlled radio and TV but left the press free: Mugabe has a tight grip on *all* the media.

Has nothing been achieved? At the end of 1989 the **Times** leader reviewed Mugabe's ten years in office.

---

4. Statement of WCC's Central Committee, August 1980, p.9 "South Africa in Crisis" (WCC 1983).
5. p.143 "World Conference on Church and Society": official report (WCC 1967).

"Before independence half of all farmland, which included the best quality areas, was reserved for white settlers. Today about a third of the available land is still owned by Zimbabwe's 4,000 white farmers ... (who) provide 80% of marketable output and most of the vital export crops, such as tobacco, beef and soya beans. Their precipitate replacement by black farmers would be an economic disaster."[6]

When Mugabe became prime minister, says the **Times**, he promised to resettle 162,000 black families within five years on idle land. Ten years later he has resettled only 52,000 families and the land for these has been bought with British aid funds. There is not enough land to absorb the 250,000 black youths who leave school every year and are not much interested in farming anyway. Corruption scandals and worsening economic problems are causing dissatisfaction with the government.

All this and much else, according to the **Times**. And it adds a warning: in April 1990 the life of the British constitution expires and Mugabe will be free to do as he pleases. His ZANU party is committed to a "victory of socialism over capitalism" and a Marxist-Leninist one-party state so Zimbabwe could grow even more like Ceausescu's Romania.

At its first Assembly in Amsterdam in 1948 the WCC described the kind of society for which we should strive:
"A responsible society is one where freedom is the freedom of men who acknowledge responsibility to justice and public order, and where those who hold political authority or economic power are responsible for its exercise to God and the people whose welfare is affected by it."[7]

The tyranny of a black Marxist government is hardly a step towards that "responsible society" and may conceivably be worse than a white government free, as Rhodesia always was, from apartheid. The WCC's policy of backing Marxist terrorists may be the quickest way of toppling white governments in Africa: what is not clear is how it benefits ordinary black people.

---

6. **Times**, 26th December 1989.
7. quoted on p.14 "Amsterdam to Nairobi", Ernest W. Lefever (1979).

Chapter XIII

SWAPO: END OF A MYTH

MR Issaacks, a former SWAPO official, showed reporters weals on his back which he said were sustained while being tortured. "They hanged me upside down, then ten chaps hit me with a stick at the same time. When that failed to make me talk I was buried alive."

A spokesman for the released prisoners, Othniel Kaakunga, had been a member of the SWAPO Politburo for ten years. He said: "In the camps prisoners were put in holes in the ground; one woman spent five years in a hole. One man had been forced to sit on a smouldering tree stump. Women were hung up in the trees by their ankles."

Freed prisoner, Mr Japhet Isaac, an ex-SWAPO representative to the United Nations, said he was seized in May 1986, accused of spying and imprisoned without trial. He said he was forced to confess after being hung upside down, beaten with sticks and buried alive. "The choice was clear; either confess or die" he said.

Lisa Nganyone worked for SWAPO as a secretary: "The prisoners were kept in pits dug deep into the ground, like being in a cage. During the day they had to work so hard until they were exhausted: digging ditches, hauling water, chopping wood. At nights they had to go back to these holes in the ground. They live there in the most cramped conditions, men and women. The stench is unbelievable, the latrines are only emptied once a week."[1]

You might assume, reading these statements by members of SWAPO—South-West African People's Organisation—that their

---

1. These passages are taken from booklets published by the International Society for Human Rights, 27 Old Gloucester Street, London, WC1N 3XX. Taken together they are the most comprehensive record of the camps and of ISHR's efforts to make the facts known that has yet been published.
"Human Rights in Conflict" (1985).
"Swapo, the Church and Human Rights" (1986)
"Detained, Disappeared, Murdered—Human Rights Abuses in SWAPO Camps in Angola and Zambia" (1988)
"No Escape From Misery?" (1989)

torturers were South Africans. You would be mistaken. Their torturers were *their own people,* fellow Namibians and fellow members of SWAPO. They were accused, quite irrationally, of being South African spies and they were beaten for days, weeks, months, until they "confessed". They were men and women who had left Namibia for the SWAPO refugee camps across the border in Angola. They were all loyal to SWAPO and could not account for their ill-treatment. Some thought that Sam Nujoma, SWAPO's leader, was getting rid of the more educated members who wanted to reform SWAPO's undemocratic structure. Others said it was a tribal thing, SWAPO leaders being mostly from the Cvambo tribe.

In mid-1989 some of the prisoners began returning to Namibia. Their release was not due to any change of heart on Nujoma's part: he wanted SWAPO to enter for the United Nations-supervised elections at the end of the year and to do so he had first to release his prisoners. By August 1989 only 156 had returned. We have lists of nearly 1,000 prisoners either dead or missing. There may be many more still alive in the camps. No one knows. And very few people care.

The existence of SWAPO's concentration camps is not new: it has been known since the early 1980s. Painstaking research has been done by the International Society for Human Rights which began publishing its findings in 1985. But the Society's investigations have been hampered by some organisations that might have been expected to show most concern for its humanitarian work: the World Council of Churches (WCC), the Lutheran World Federation (LWF), the United Nations High Commissioner for Refugees (UNHCR), the Namibia Council of Churches (NCC), the British Council of Churches (BCC). By refusing co-operation, by deliberate silence and, in some instances, by active opposition, these bodies, that should have been the allies of SWAPO's victims, sided with their tormentors. Even when the facts were established beyond reasonable doubt they continued their public campaigns in support of SWAPO as if its reputation were still undamaged. The WCC, which has given over £1 million to SWAPO since 1970, made a further grant in September 1989 *after* the statements by SWAPO prisoners quoted above had appeared in leading European newspapers. "We are deeply saddened by these reports" said Emilio Castro, the WCC's General Secretary, "but we believe SWAPO still remains the symbol of hope for the Namibian people".[2]

This attachment to SWAPO, right or wrong, is part of the political mythology of leftist Christians: SWAPO is cast in the role of St. George in shining armour slaying the fearsome dragon of South Africa. John Carlin went to Namibia to question the returning SWAPO prisoners and in an article entitled "Torture Under Freedom's Flag" wrote this:

"For many years there has been a sort of international conspiracy to project SWAPO, the most pampered 'freedom fighters' the world has seen, as the incarnation of all that is fine and noble and heroic. They were fighting South Africa. They were black. They were the underdogs. They were sacrosanct. There was no need to examine the detail, the fact that they were a far-from democratic organisation run along Stalinist lines of command; that on the battlefield they were ineffectual; that they milked huge amounts of money from international organisations, for much of which they have been unable to account. Worst of all, no one noticed, or chose to notice, the atrocities they were committing against their own followers".[3]

The churches' surrender to these great moral simplicities means that they have functioned as propaganda organs for SWAPO. Canon George Austin, who at the time was a member of the British Council of Churches' Assembly writes:

"At a meeting of the Assembly in 1977 a paper was produced on Namibia, intended to be a factual guide for British church-people ... It was pointed out forcibly by Assembly members of widely differing political standpoints that the paper was seriously lacking in balance. It made no mention of the real attempts that had been made to dismantle certain aspects of apartheid in Namibia; it totally ignored all non-white moderate political groups who opposed the South African government ... making it appear that the only opposition came from SWAPO; and it made no reference to the SWAPO moderates detained in Zambia and Tanzania. One member, well-known for his support for the WCC's Program to

---

2. The **Citizen** newspaper, 23rd September 1989.
3. John Carlin, The **Independent**, 18th September 1989.

Combat Racism, had while visiting Tanzania made unsuccessful representations for the release of the detainees, and he was able to speak also with first-hand knowledge of schoolchildren abducted from Namibia with promises of university education, then detained in Zambia because they refused to become guerrillas. Yet the 'information' paper was still published in its original unbalanced form, and a member of the BCC staff commented afterwards to one critic that the pressure from his Board was often 'Please, DON'T try to be balanced in what you produce'!"[4]

Notice that Canon Austin says that the BCC paper "made no reference to the SWAPO moderates detained in Zambia and Tanzania". They were detained in 1976, the year before the BCC Assembly meeting, and the facts were widely publicised at the time. Andreas Shipanga, a co-founder of SWAPO, had gone to Lusaka in Zambia for a SWAPO congress. Sam Nujoma, SWAPO's autocratic leader, knowing that Shipanga wanted the party run in a more democratic manner, arrested his rival and all his supporters and deported them to prisons in Tanzania. Shipanga was eventually released and now leads a new party inside Namibia, SWAPO-Democrats.[5]

Sam Nujoma's contempt for democracy is to be expected from the leader of a party committed to Marxist-Leninism. Its 1976 policy statement spoke of "a classless, non-exploitative society based on scientific socialist ideals" with the government having "control over the means of production and distribution".

In 1978 a TV interviewer asked Nujoma if he would be satisfied by an end to racial discrimination and the introduction of black majority rule in Namibia. Nujoma replied with commendable frankness: "We are not fighting against discrimination as such ... We are not fighting even for majority rule. We are fighting to seize power in Namibia for the benefit of the Namibian people. We are revolutionaries ... You can talk to Kapuuo, Kerina and all those reactionaries about majority rule and not to SWAPO".[6]

---

4. George Austin, p.16, "WCC's Program to Combat Racism" (1979)
5. Sue Armstrong, "In Search of Freedom: Andreas Shipanga's Story" (Ashanti Publishing 1989)
6. p.31, "South West Africa" (Dept. of Information, South African Embassy, London, No date)

Chief Clemens Kapuuo of the Herero people, derisively mentioned by Nujoma, was a widely respected politician in Namibia, tipped as a future president when the country achieved independence. He had no time for SWAPO or its methods. In a letter to the **Times** newspaper in 1975 he had written: "SWAPO has boycotted elections in Namibia while yet claiming to be 'sole legitimate representative of the people'. I am determined that the South African government must leave our country. I am equally determined not to exchange their tyranny for another. I believe that most ordinary members of SWAPO do not share the taste which some of their leaders have for violence and international terrorism ... It is by civilised and diplomatic means, not through violence or terrorism that the true friends of Namibia will best serve its people".[7] Four weeks after Sam Nujumo's TV interview, Chief Kapuuo was shot dead outside his house by a SWAPO gunman using a Russian automatic pistol.

Although there is, as far as I know, no record of the churches having murdered any of the democratic party leaders in Namibia, they certainly treat them as if they did not exist. In 1983 the Archbishop of Canterbury sent a delegation to Namibia led by Mr Terry Waite. The report that subsequently appeared contains a "Brief History" of Namibia. It has half a page on SWAPO but not one of the six democratic parties is mentioned. Clearly church leaders do not share Chief Kapuuo's preference for "civilised and diplomatic" means of achieving independence. The report is very soft on SWAPO claiming that the people are more afraid of the South African Defence Force (SADF) than of SWAPO. The evidence for this consists of eleven pages, nearly two-thirds of the report, entitled "What We Heard", listing brief remarks, often single sentences, made by a variety of unnamed people and overheard by the delegation. "We have not just chosen extracts with which we agree" says the report. Yet out of 109 remarks, 23 are critical of the SADF and only two are critical of SWAPO. This enables the report to conclude that "the people fear the army and the Koevoet far more than they fear SWAPO".[8] This is a surprising conclusion that receives little support from figures:

---

7. **Times** newspaper, 31st December 1975.
8. p.24, "Namibia: A Report to the Archbishop of Canterbury by the Anglican Delegation" (1984)

perhaps this is why no figures appear in the report. They were available to the delegation as they are to anyone who cares to ask the Administrator-General for them. These show that in the nine months preceding the delegation's visit, 21 members of the SADF were tried in the civil (not military) courts for the following crimes against civilians: murder (5), assault (9), rape (3), culpable homicide (1), theft (3). Two were found not guilty and the rest were sentenced, one murderer receiving 15 years in prison. In the same nine months in cross-border strikes, SWAPO committed the following crimes against civilians: 28 murders; 15 killed and 28 injured in landmine explosions; 171 abductions. None of SWAPO's criminals were brought to trial.

The report does not mention SWAPO's abductions but it does mention the SADF's: it does not mention SWAPO's tortures and beatings but it does the SADF's: it does not mention SWAPO "spreading distrust by informers" but it does the SADF. These omissions enable it to conclude: "The occupation by the SADF in the name of 'protecting' the people of Namibia is causing hardship, distress, fear and loss of life".

The Anglicans' visit to Namibia in October 1983 overlapped a visit by an All-Party Parliamentary Group from Westminster made up of two Labour Lords and three Conservative MPs. In their report they discuss the charge of "systematic torture and oppression" levelled at the SADF by "SWAPO and its allies". They reasonably say: "Our own security forces have defied the Queensbury Rules on occasion, and we have no doubt that similar incidents occur in Namibia. The question is: Is such wrongdoing part of the Government's official strategy, or can the victims expect to obtain redress through the courts? We have seen many reports—in local newspapers and elsewhere—of court cases leading to severe penalties for Security Force and Koevoet personnel who ignore the rules. We have concluded that ill-treatment *does* regrettably take place from time to time, but that it is by no means 'institutionalised' ".

In January 1985 another group of MPs, members of the All-Party Namibia Group, visited Namibia and subsequently reported their findings. They met a wide variety of people and groups including the Namibian Council of Churches (NCC), to which the Anglican, Lutheran, Roman Catholic and Methodist Churches all belong. This body raised the question of alleged atrocities by the SADF and the group put these charges to the Administrator-General. They came to the same conclusions as the previous parliamentary group but attached to their report a long appendix by the A-G including full details of all criminal charges brought against members of the SADF over a two-and-a-half year period. The report ends with an appeal to SWAPO "to end its use of violence in the belief that SWAPO's attempts to promote revolution delay independence for Namibia".

The MPs comments on their meeting with the NCC are revealing: "We noted that criticisms of the actions of the SADF were not matched by criticism of the violent atrocities committed by SWAPO. Namibians regard the NCC as leaning towards support for SWAPO. Certainly nothing was said by the NCC to dispel this view". The MPs were not as well briefed for their visit as they might have been: they did not know that NCC and SWAPO personnel are, it seems, interchangeable. Dr Abisai Shejavali, NCC's General Secretary, is a leading member of SWAPO and represents it at international conferences: Daniel Tjongarero, NCC Director of Communications is a Vice-president of SWAPO and Chairman of SWAPO's internal wing: Frans Kambangula is Transport Officer for NCC and SWAPO Executive Committee member with responsibility for transport: Immanuel Ngatijzeko is NCC's Treasurer and a SWAPO Executive member: Nora Chase, NCC's Education Secretary was a SWAPO delegate at the Lusaka talks in 1984. According to the sworn testimony of former NCC employees and SWAPO members, the NCC has a close working relationship with SWAPO and the two bodies are "inseparably linked".[9]

The MPs also met Bishop Kauluma, the Anglican Bishop of Namibia, and Father Bruno, the Dean of Windhoek. In their report they say: "Some of us were surprised by the Anglican Church in Namibia's apparent open commitment to SWAPO and that it has little confidence in members of the other internal parties. We found this to be a sad reflection on the Anglican Church and we were surprised to hear it described as 'the religious wing of SWAPO'. Apparently the Bishop and the Dean did not seem

---

9. "SWAPO, the Church and Human Rights" (ISHR, 1986)

prepared to give any credit to those in Namibia who have been working for the necessary changes". The MPs discussed violence with Anglican and Roman Catholic leaders and found "a marked difference of emphasis . . . the Anglican Church appeared to encourage violence".

The contrast of views afforded by the reports of the MPs and the report of the Anglican Delegation is too obvious to need comment: they agree on one point only—the generous support given by the churches to SWAPO. The Anglican report boasts of it: "SWAPO has overwhelming support, not least from the mainline churches and their leaders. SWAPO is reported to include many committed members of the Christian Church throughout the country . . ." (p.25, "Namibia"). The different churches that are members of the NCC give common support to SWAPO. Divided doctrinally, they are united politically.

A network of ecclesiastical SWAPO-support groups spreads out from the WCC's headquarters in Geneva through the NCC and the national councils of churches in other countries. All of them are linked constitutionally with the WCC and promote its policies. We have already seen (p.3 above) how the British Council of Churches produces propaganda for SWAPO's cause: Christian Aid, a department of the BCC, does its bit by sending large sums of money to the NCC—£123,000 in the year ending July 1985. The Namibian Communications Centre is in Manchester, its chairman Bishop Booth-Clibborn. SWAPO's European headquarters are in London. Tieing in with this network are innumerable small but active groups of Christian socialists and Christian peace movements, the latter always keen to support terrorist groups like SWAPO. Since the BCC commands the support of all main churches in Britain its power to shape opinion is very considerable. The same is true of the national councils of churches in other European countries. At intervals all these councils send their Africa Secretaries to meet SWAPO representatives to agree a common policy.

Working in this way the churches have been largely responsible for creating and sustaining the myth of SWAPO as the bringer of light to darkest Africa. They have worked well and woven a seamless garment of propaganda: it must have received many a nod of approval from the virtuosi of the art in Moscow. When it was threatened by publication of the facts about SWAPO's camps the churches stood firm, the network responding protectively with lies, deceits, prevarication and circumspect silences. In 1986 the International Society for Human Rights (ISHR) asked the BCC to take action in defence of SWAPO's prisoners. To date the only reaction from the BCC has been to reaffirm its "solidarity" with the Namibian church leaders. But since the Namibian churches are members of the NCC which is staffed, as we have seen, by SWAPO officials, this can only mean solidarity with SWAPO. In other words, the BCC allies itself with the torturers not the tortured. The latest of many appeals to the BCC from the ISHR was in September 1989. The **Church Times** reported the BCC's General Secretary as saying: "We will respond but not with enormous urgency".[10] Five months later, as I write this chapter, the ISHR tells me there has still been no response.

The BCC follows the bad example of SWAPO's leaders and the General Secretary of the United Nations, none of whom has answered any of ISHR's letters. The UN has an interest in perpetuating the SWAPO myth. Since its foundation in 1945 the UN has contested South Africa's right to exercise the mandate over South West Africa (Namibia) given to it by the League of Nations after the First World War. In 1966 the UN arbitrarily "terminated" the mandate and declared South Africa's presence illegal. It made itself responsible for the territory and appointed a Commissioner for Namibia, as it now called it, Mr Sean MacBride, a former IRA chief-of-staff. In 1975 the UN declared SWAPO "the sole and authentic representative of the people of Namibia". This was an obvious fiction since SWAPO had never submitted its popularity to the test of the polls, having boycotted every election ever held in Namibia. It had long ago left Namibia for military camps in Angola. Armed by Soviet-bloc countries and trained by Cuban combat troops it carried out raids from these bases across the border into Namibia.

In choosing SWAPO as "sole representative" of the Namibian people, the UN was deliberately ignoring the political parties in Namibia that had resisted the temptation to resort to violence and were patiently working for reform and independence by

---

10. **Church Times**, 15th September 1989.

democractic means. Snubbed by the UN and sneered at by Sam Nujoma as "puppet politicians", they nevertheless passed a law abolishing apartheid in 1978 which was so effectively implemented that both the Parliamentary Groups that visited Namibia noted the absence of racial discrimination. The Anglican Delegation, perhaps unwilling to admit that any improvements could be brought about except by violence, spoke gloomily of "the shadow of apartheid cast over the country".

The UN is as guilty as the churches in choosing to ignore the SWAPO victims. The United Nations High Commissioner for Refugees was not directly responsible for conditions in the SWAPO camps but could have put pressure on SWAPO leaders to allow UNHCR officials to inspect: he chose not to do so. As SWAPO had already refused to allow the International Red Cross into the camps this meant that the camps would remain closed to neutral observers. But was UNHCR neutral? Dr Reinhard Gnauck, director of ISHR, found that the High Commissioner "contributed actively" to the campaign to conceal SWAPO's crimes and thwart aid to the victims. Letters to the UNHCR went unanswered and the same telex was sent three times in as many months without evoking any response. Although full documentation of the case against SWAPO had been personally handed to the UNHCR in Geneva, representatives of UNHCR were still saying, as late as April 1989, that they knew nothing about it. Yet UNHCR had been the "operational partner" of SWAPO in Angola and Zambia for twenty years, handing over to SWAPO vast sums of money and material goods to be used for the relief of refugees from Namibia. Is it credible that UNHCR knew nothing of what was going on inside the camps?

John Carlin's article on the returned SWAPO prisoners, from which I have already quoted, ends with a visit to an old friend of his in Windhoek who had been a loyal SWAPO activist for 20 years. He was now a changed man: he had been talking to the SWAPO prisoners.

"Such is his disgust and the extent of his fear of SWAPO winning the two-thirds majority in the November election necessary to assume full power, that, to my amazement, he told me, with grave conviction: 'If SWAPO wins two-thirds I shall be out of here and living in South Africa by the end of the year'. My friend, who has fought against apartheid all his life, is not white."[11]

The elections have now been held and to many people's relief SWAPO polled only 57% of the votes. So Carlin's friend can stay on in Namibia. Perhaps SWAPO will be required to consult with the other parties in drawing up a constitution prior to independence. But for how long will it be content to share power with those it has always regarded as the puppets of South Africa? Falsely acclaimed by the United Nations as the "sole representative of the Namibian people", is it likely to let a handful of votes stand between it and absolute power? And knowing what we do of Sam Nujoma's treatment of dissidents in his own party, how tolerant will he be of those who oppose him in other parties? These are questions only the future can answer. But if I were Mr Carlin's friend, I think I'd pack my bag.

---

11. see 3 above.

Chapter XIV

VIOLENCE AND THE CHURCHES IN SOUTH AFRICA

AS I write this, Nelson Mandela, one of the leaders of the African National Congress (ANC), is on a triumphal fund-raising tour of the West's capital cities. Released from prison, he arrived in New York where a million people gave him a ticker-tape welcome. In Washington he gave an address to Congress: in the past only two other foreign private citizens have been accorded this privilege. In Rome he had a twenty-five minute private audience with the Pope who obligingly blessed the ANC's "initiatives". Mr Mandela responded by urging His Holiness to support sanctions against South Africa.[1]

An occasional discordant note has been struck by some journalists who remind us that Mandela has praised Castro's Cuba for its "love for human rights and liberty" and has spoken of Colonel Gaddafi as "a comrade-in-arms".[2] The **Sunday Telegraph** published an interview with Mandela's first wife Evelyn, whom he abandoned together with their four children. The same paper carried an article proving links between the ANC and the IRA.[3] At least one journalist noticed the irony of Mandela arriving in Kenya just as President Moi was energetically suppressing demands for democratic elections: at least twenty people had been killed in clashes with the security forces. The wives of seven political detainees asked Mandela to intervene on behalf of their husbands but he seems to have kept a diplomatic silence. Except that the government was black instead of white it was really quite like South Africa.[4]

But none of this was allowed to spoil the festive mood. Neatly-suited, formal and dignified, Nelson Mandela performed on the world's stage like an elder statesman. A figure of mythic stature in the folk-lore of the political left, he had at last come into his

---

1. **Daily Telegraph** 16th June 1990
2. **Daily Telegraph** 29th June 1990
3. **Sunday Telegraph** 25th February 1990 and 1st July 1990
4. **Daily Telegraph** 14th July 1990

own. Released after 27 years in prison, the occasion was hailed by the Rev Frank Chikane, secretary-general of the South African Council of Churches (SACC), as equivalent to the second coming of Christ. Less extravagantly, Archbishop Tutu assures us that Mandela will be South Africa's first black Prime Minister. The world is not unused to terrorists who come in from the bush to assume the dignities of heads of state: Kenyatta, Mugabe, Shamir, Begin, Machel . . . it's a familiar ladder of promotion. But before Mandela and the ANC disappear altogether from view behind the screens of respectability it is as well to recall a few facts.

The ANC, founded in 1912, was at first a gentlemanly affair—a group of black lawyers intent on arguing a case for civil rights. Its leader was a Zulu, Dr Seme, who had studied law at Oxford and the Middle Temple. But gradually it attracted men of a different stamp. In 1936 a communist, J. B. Marks, became its secretary-general. Marks had been trained in Moscow and went back there to die: he was rewarded by being buried with full soviet honours. In 1943 a group of young blacks who wanted to give the ANC a sharper edge founded the ANC's Youth League: they included Mandela, Walter Sisulu and Oliver Tambo. All three were soon on the ANC's national executive and in 1949 Sisulu became its secretary-general. In the same year they persuaded the ANC to approve a massive campaign of civil disobedience, strikes and boycotts. The following year the Suppression of Communism Act drove the Communist Party underground, many of its members joining the ANC.

In 1961 Mandela addressed a secret meeting of the ANC's national executive. He argued that every attempt to achieve their ends by demonstrations and strikes had been defeated by government counter-action. The time had come to abandon non-violence for a campaign of sabotage and insurrection. His views were approved and the ANC's military wing, Umkhonto we Sizwe, the Spear of the Nation, was formed. Money provided by the Communist Party bought a remote farmstead at Rivonia, near Johannesburg, used as Umkhonto's headquarters. Over the next eighteen months some two hundred acts of sabotage against railways and public buildings were carried out and some black policemen—"Government stooges"—were attacked.

The remote farmstead had not escaped the attention of the police and eventually Mandela, Sisulu and eight others were charged with sabotage and conspiring to cause violent revolution. The trial lasted eight months during which it turned out that Mandela had spent six months touring African states raising money for arms. He had trained in sabotage and guerilla warfare and arranged the same training for 300 young ANC recruits. Documents seized at the farmstead included 106 maps marked with targets for attack including "police stations, post offices, Black Administration offices, the houses of Black policemen and administrators, electric power stations, pylons, railway lines, signal boxes, and telephone lines and cables."[5] Another document headed "Production Requirements" listed:

210,000 hand grenades
48,000 anti-personnel mines
1,500 devices for bombs
144 tons of ammonium nitrate
21 tons of aluminium powder
15 tons of black powder.[6]

Experts testified that these quantities were sufficient to blow up the city of Johannesburg. Mandela and his friends were all sentenced to life imprisonment. The defendants' legal costs were met by Canon Collins' Defence and Aid Fund in London.[7]

The ANC was now declared an illegal organisation and its leaders, if not in prison, retreated into exile. In Tanzania they set up a camp for training young recruits in guerilla warfare; the most talented were sent for special tuition in Soviet Russia and East Germany. A new Revolutionary Council was formed led by Oliver Tambo, who had at one time intended becoming an Anglican priest—"and a very fine priest he would have made" according to Canon Collins[8]—Yusuf Dadoo, a leading communist, and Joe Slovo, a prominent member of the Communist Party and chief of staff of Umkhonto. By infiltrating saboteurs across the South African border hundreds of targets were attacked. The most sophisticated operations included planting bombs that caused

---

5. H. H. W. de Villiers, "Rivonia: Operation Mayibuye" p.73, (Johannesburg, 1964)
6. Ibid. p.71.
7. Canon John Collins, "Faith Under Fire" p.229, (London, 1966).
8. Ibid. p.210.

serious damage to a nuclear reactor, destroying fuel storage tanks at a Sasol plant and firing rockets at a military base. Uglier incidents are typified by the attack by three ANC terrorists on the Volkskas Bank in Pretoria in 1980. Armed with hand-grenades and Kalashnikov rifles they took 25 hostages. Among their demands was the immediate release of Mandela. To enforce these they shot dead a girl bank clerk. When police attacked, the terrorists threw a hand-grenade amongst the hostages killing one woman and wounding eleven others.[9] In May 1983 a car-bomb exploded in Pretoria killing sixteen people and wounding over 200. It was by far the worst incident of its kind.

In 1970 the WCC began making annual grants of money to the ANC which have continued to the present day—a total of more than £400,000. But far more important than money is the fact that the ANC, whose methods are no different to those of the IRA, has gained moral respectability from the WCC's support. The WCC calls the ANC a "liberation movement" and promotes a wholly false picture of an amiably democratic body fully entitled to Christian approval. Ordinary members of churches, asked if there are ever circumstances in which the use of car bombs are justified, confidently answer no. When given the facts about the WCC's church support for the ANC they are incredulous. That is a measure of how successfully the WCC has veiled the less attractive features of the ANC to make it acceptable to liberal Christians.

Two months after the Pretoria car bomb the WCC's 1983 Assembly opened in Vancouver. Over 1,000 delegates and observers attended with nearly as many reporters from the press, radio and TV in train. The Assembly condemned "the enormous suffering" caused by apartheid: "restriction of movement, arbitrary arrests, detention without trial, torture and death have become an institutionalized way of intimidating black people . . . these policies . . . create an extremely explosive climate . . . a church . . . which seeks to proclaim the liberating Gospel and the divine demand for justice cannot avoid a confrontation with the government . . . In confessing the faith it is impossible in South

---

9. Henry R. Pike, "A History of Communism in South Africa" p.491, (South Africa, 1985)

Africa not to call for a fundamental change in the political, social and economic order of the country".[10] The Assembly called on the churches "to intensify their witness against apartheid and the continuing oppression in South Africa and to deepen their solidarity with the liberation movements".[11]

The Assembly's condemnation of violence by the South African government was not matched by any condemnation of violence by the ANC. It recorded its "abhorrence of all forms of violence" but still made no mention of the ANC. This partiality is characteristic of the WCC. If moral censure is applied it must be applied even-handedly. It is easy to see why it is not. The passage I have quoted makes it plain that the churches must, according to the WCC, become the allies of the ANC: to do otherwise is to abandon the Gospel. Combatants do not wish to be reminded that even in war there are moral constraints. Criticism of the enemy is welcome but not of one's allies. The WCC has made the fatal error of identifying the Gospel with a political programme: however worthy it may seem to strive for a society in which democratic rights are accorded to all regardless of colour, this is not what the Gospel is about. In the end it is not politics which is sanctified but the Gospel which is politicised by being made to serve the ambitions of a secular creed.

The history of the ANC illustrates the dangers that attend the use of violence by political campaigners. The justification is always that because attempts to negotiate have repeatedly failed there is no alternative but violence. "Thirty years of my life have been spent knocking in vain, patiently, moderately and modestly at a closed and barred door."[12] Albert Luthuli wrote those famous words in 1952 when he became President of the ANC. But he was justifying not violence but non-violent civil disobedience as "the only non-revolutionary, legitimate and humane way" to further his aspirations. Luthuli was a Christian of great nobility of character but he was a liberal and a pacifist whose grasp of political reality was consequently weak. Long before he died the ANC had become contemptuous of his "legitimate and humane way". When Oliver

---

10. David Gill ed. Official Report of WCC's Vancouver Assembly, p.152, (Geneva, 1983).
11. Ibid. pp.155-6
12. Albert Luthuli, "Let My People Go" p.235, (London, 1962)

Tambo succeeded him in 1967 the pretence of non-violence had long since been dropped. The sporadic forays into South Africa, which were all the exiled ANC could now undertake, were frustratingly modest. Something bigger and more dramatic was needed to appease the revolutionary zeal. Non-violence had been discarded in favour of violence but neither had succeeded in forcing concessions from the government. The revolutionary always believes that *more* violence will achieve what violence has so far failed to achieve. Like an addictive drug, violence is taken in ever-larger doses. The 1980s saw the start of a new and more violent campaign in the black townships that was to make "necklacing" a household word. Luthuli's words were still used to justify behaviour that he would have found repugnant.

Whether the United Democratic Front was founded in 1983 by the ANC or by Dr Allan Boesak, president of the World Alliance of Reformed Churches, is a matter for dispute: it matters little since its policies are the same as the ANC's, it functions as the "internal arm" of the ANC in exile, and most of its office-holders have been members of the ANC or the South African Communist Party (SACP). The UDF's membership totals some 600 groups, about half of them youth and student organizations. Its aim is to destroy the black administration in the townships and make them ungovernable. Street committees are then set up to run the townships on the model of revolutionary communes. The methods used by the UDF are made plain in the following reports of what happened in the black townships of the Vaal Triangle in March 1984.[13]

A number of community organizations called a strike and a school boycott to protest against rent increases. An Anglican priest, the Rev Jeff Moselane, was one of the leading agitators and was later arrested. Shortly afterwards—"Gangs of armed youths marched from school to school, including primary schools, ordering the pupils onto the streets. Flanked by hundreds of excited children, the leaders headed for the liquor stores which were plundered and set alight. The burned body of a man was later found

---

13. **Signposts**, "A digest of researched information for concerned Christians", ed by Edward Cain, Vol.3: No.5: 1984. (PO Box 26148, Arcadia 0007, South Africa).

in one. Made reckless by alcohol, the mobs now turned to their real targets, the homes and properties of the 'stooges' and 'sellouts'—the mayors, community councillors and policemen. In Evaton a mob of 2,000 on a 'protest march' surrounded the house of Councillor Caesar Motjeane shouting 'Here's the dog's place'. A long stick wrapped in cloth and doused in inflammable liquid was used to set his house and car alight. He was dragged from his house and killed while the crowd ululated with joy. Mr Dutch Diphoko, deputy mayor of Evaton and a business man was trapped when a huge crowd surrounded his house. He was stoned and his home set alight. He shot two of his attackers but died the following day in hospital. Two people were burned to death when rioters set fire to the home of a Sebokeng councillor. Two others died after being trapped in vehicles set alight. Mr J. Chakane of the Lekoa Town Council was brutally attacked by the mob outside his home, dying a week later. The mayor of Lekoa narrowly escaped death when he was attacked outside his home: the shopping centre he owned was destroyed.

By the end of the day the riots left most of the homes of Vaal councillors in irreparable ruins. In response to a call for all councillors to resign, several resigned and others went into hiding.

The following day the mobs turned on the Indian families in Evaton and burned their homes and businesses. Their losses were estimated at more than £8 million and included 40 homes and shops, a car mart, several surgeries and a clinic offering free medical assistance. Hundreds of poor people were thus deprived of the treatment they had been receiving. An Indian relief committee had given free food parcels and clothing to Evaton's destitute blacks every week.

The townships were totally devastated by the riots. Every shop had been destroyed and buses only operated on the outskirts. It should be noted that the violence took place in model townships which had a strong black middle class which had not complained about the black councillors. A week after the riots a journalist on the Johannesburg **Star** tried to speak to Vaal councillors but found they were all still in hiding. When asked to comment on the riots a mayor said: 'I would not like to. The moment you comment they come and bomb your house. The quieter, the better'.

According to Mr D. C. Ganz, chief director of the Orange Vaal

Development Board, 'Most meetings where this fiasco was planned took place in houses and churches in the Triangle with the wholehearted co-operation and direction of the ministers involved. In these meetings in churches the burning of shops and driving out of community council members was planned. UDF speakers were presented to promote the matter. The issue of rent increases was just used as a smoke screen by the agitators' ''.

Following the Vaal riots 19 leaders of the UDF were arrested and charged with treason, sedition and murder. It was the longest trial in South African legal history, lasting over three years. It produced evidence to support the view of Mr Ganz that the churches were active in organising and inciting the riots. One of the accused was Tom Manthata who at one time studied for the Catholic priesthood but was expelled for his political activities. At the time of the riots he was a field worker for the South African Council of Churches (SACC), the equivalent in South Africa of our former BCC. Desmond Tutu, SACC's general secretary, sent him to the Vaal townships some months before the riots began because he would have a "rational, calming influence" on a situation of rising tension. He appears to have had the opposite effect when he addressed a meeting in an Anglican church hall, ten days before the riot began, and vehemently attacked town councillors saying they should be attacked with stones and set alight if they refused to resign. Manthata was sentenced to six years imprisonment. The Bishop described him as "a highly responsible and trusted member of my staff."[14]

Another of the UDF leaders, Moses Chikane, was jailed for ten years. Before becoming an official of the UDF he worked on church and community projects for the Independent Ministers Association. He is the elder brother of the Rev Frank Chikane who gave the opening speech at the launch of UDF and was a UDF official before succeeding Desmond Tutu as general secretary of SACC.

On 8th January 1987 many South African newspapers carried full-page advertisements demanding the unbanning of the ANC. The advertisements were placed jointly by SACC and the UDF: in some papers they were joined by the Catholic Bishops'

---

14. **Signposts,** Vol.8: No.1: 1989.

Conference. SACC has always supported the ANC. In May of the same year the WCC held a conference in Lusaka, Zambia. The ANC has its headquarters in Lusaka and this was the 75th year of its founding. For the first time the leaders of liberation movements were invited to attend as delegates. Oliver Tambo, President of the ANC spoke against a back-drop of ANC posters and flags. Sam Nujoma spoke for SWAPO and Dr Beyers Naude spoke for SACC. At the end of the conference the delegates issued the Lusaka Statement which in part reads:

"We affirm the unquestionable right of the people of Namibia and South Africa to secure justice and peace through the liberation movements . . . We recognise that the nature of the South African regime . . . compels the movements to use force along with the other means to end oppression. We call upon the churches and the international community to give this affirmation practical effect in the struggle for liberation and to strengthen their contacts with the liberation movements. We commit ourselves to further the cause of unity in our own churches, and in our ministry to the movements of liberation operating to bring to an end the illegitimate regime in South Africa and Namibia".[15]

A few weeks later SACC held its national conference and under the guidance of its secretary-general Dr Naude endorsed the Lusaka Statement by seven votes to one. Most delegates had no doubt that in doing so SACC had formally justified the use of violence by the ANC and SWAPO.

Encouraged by the approval of church leaders, the UDF/ANC intensified the violence in the black townships. In April 1986 at a rally at Munsieville, Winnie Mandela had told an assembly of many hundreds of blacks: "Together, hand-in-hand with our boxes of matches and our necklaces we shall liberate this country". Father Arthur Lewis writes: "Apart from crucifixion, which took longer, the necklace is the most hideous form of execution invented by man. The victim, limbs bound, has a petrol-filled tyre slung round his neck. As it is lit enormous temperatures are generated and flesh and rubber are fused together as a pathetic remnant of humanity screams and writhes in agony—and anguished friends stand by helplessly. Of nearly 800 Africans burned to death by ANC

---

15. quoted in **Signposts**, Vol.6: No.4: 1987

supporters from 1984 till 1989 about half died by necklacing".[16] In the same month that Mrs Mandela made her infamous remark, the President of South Africa, P. W. Botha, gave the following figures to the House of Delegates:

"From the start of the unrest in September 1984 until yesterday, 508 people, mostly moderate blacks, were brutally murdered by radical blacks, mostly by the necklace method. In addition 439 blacks were killed during the same period by fellow blacks in so-called tribal or faction fighting, which has nothing whatever to do with so-called apartheid, or, for that matter, politics. In the same period no less than 1,417 black-owned businesses, 4,435 private homes (including 814 homes of black policemen), 28 churches, 54 community centres, several hundred schools and a number of clinics—all serving the black community—were either totally destroyed or badly damaged by petrol bombs or other forms of arson or attacks. In addition several thousand private vehicles—again black-owned—were destroyed or severely damaged". (Speech to the House on 23rd April, 1986).

And, lest evidence from Mr Botha should be considered suspect, the *black* newspaper the **Sowetan** reported in its issues of the 11th and 14th April 1986 evidence of a massacre in Lebowa in the Eastern Transvaal: thirty-two bodies of black persons had all been found murdered by the necklace method. This was South Africa's worst mass murder: the 76 black youths arrested in connection with it were all members or supporters of the UDF which likes to present itself, at press conferences, as a non-violent body. The massacre was also reported in the **New York Times** which gave it no more than *two sentences* at the foot of a 14 inch column about the election of Desmond Tutu as Archbishop of Cape Town. The sub-editor's sense of priorities was nicely adjusted to the liberal conscience: blacks killing blacks is unwelcome news. Would the massacre have been given more prominence if it had been the work of the South African police?

Tutu, a Nobel Peace Prize winner, is a much more acceptable image of the black struggle for freedom. Making the award in 1984 the Nobel Committee said: "This award should be seen as a renewed recognition of the courage and heroism shown by black

---

16. Rev Arthur Lewis, "Churches in the Dark" (London, July, 1990).

South Africans in their use of peaceful methods in the struggle against apartheid."[17] Clearly the Nobel Committee had not been reading the South African newspapers.

Tutu himself performs a skilled balancing act on the question of violence: like the WCC he manages at one and the same time to be both for it and against it. He speaks of "the glorious liberation struggle" and likes to see it as analogous to the Exodus: "You must know that the victory of liberation and freedom is assured. Our God and the God of freedom and liberation will lead us out of bondage. He will lead us out of oppression and suffering and exploitation. We shall be free. About that there is no doubt. But our liberation is going to be costly. Many more will be detained. Many more will be banned. Many more will be killed. Yes, it will be costly. But we shall be free. Nothing will stop us becoming free—no police bullets, dogs, tear gas, prison, death, no nothing will stop us because God is on our side'.[18]

This sounds very much like a holy war, yet Tutu assures us that he is a man of peace. Disliking violence himself, he will not deny its use to others. Emotive words like "traitor" come easily to his lips: "Make no mistake about it, if you go over to the other side the day of reckoning will come. This is not a threat, it is just the plain truth. Blacks will never forget that you were traitors to the liberation struggle". And for the Archbishop there is no such person as a "moderate": "My friends, in a situation of injustice and oppression ... there are only two groups—the oppressed and the oppressor. There is no inbetween ... you are either oppressed or you are an oppressor". Denying the moderate's right to exist is often the first step to exterminating him.

Such attitudes characterise the Marxist revolutionary: are we really surprised when they are voiced by church leaders? Probably not. Joe Slovo, chief of the South African Communist Party, has said that Jesus would have joined the armed struggle had he lived in South Africa today. Liberation theologians put the same point with more sophistication—and tedium—but Slovo has the essence of the matter. The churches have exchanged conciliation for

---

17. quoted in **Signposts**, Vol.4: No.1: 1985.
18. Ibid. This and all the other quotations from Tutu are from this issue of **Signposts**.

confrontation because they believe God is calling them to overthrow an oppressive government.

Darril Hudson, in his magisterial study of the WCC, writes: "A striking factor in the WCC's concern for racial justice ... has been the ever-increasing acceptance of violence as a means of change ... It appears that WCC officials have moved from a policy of bending over backwards not to offend white South Africans to one of stiff-necked resistance to compromise with them ... The World Council has seemed less conciliatory and less willing to compromise than Prime Minister Vorster. It is difficult to see the ultimate goal to which this posture will lead except to awesome and bloody confrontation of the races".[19] If Hudson is right, then the World Council and its member churches which have allied themselves with the ANC, bear a very heavy burden of guilt.

---

19. Darril Hudson, "The World Council of Churches in International Affairs" pp.126 and 143, (London, 1977).

Index

Athenagoras, Archbishop, 70.
Austin, Canon George, 145.

Banks, Dennis, 89, 90.
Bath and Wells, Bishop of, 23, 49.
Bax, Martin, 115.
Beky, Bishop, 54.
Beyerhaus, Dr Peter, 135.
Birley, Sir Robert, 39.
Bishop, Fr Hugh, 44.
Blake, Dr Eugene Carson, 4, 36, 61, 86, 99, 101, 106.
Bloch, Ernst, 134.
Bois, Canon Albert du, 136.
Bonino, Jose Miguez, 135.
Booth-Clibborn, Bishop, 150.
Botha, P. W., 164.
Bourdeaux, Michael, 72, 80.
Boyle, Lord, 39.
Brezhnev, Leonid, 3, 61.
Bristol, Bishop of, 44, 54.
Brown, Robert McAfee, 129.
Burrough, Bishop Paul, 18, 22.
Butt, Ronald, 20.
Bychkov, Alexei, 81.

Camara, Archbishop Helder, 106.
Carlin, John, 145, 152.
Carmichael, Dr M., 105.
Carmichael, Stokeley, 33, 35.
Carter, Jimmy, 137.
Carter, Mark Bonham, 39.
Castro, Emilio, 123, 125.
Chalfont, Lord, 14.
Chapman, Sydney, 85.
Chase, Louis, 51.
Chikane, Revd Frank, 156, 162.
Cho, Dr, 113.
Clark, Dr Colin, 115.
Coggan, Dr, Archbishop of Canterbury, 14, 21, 33, 43.
Collins, Canon John, 106, 157.
Conquest, Robert, 29.
Costa, John da, Dean of Salisbury, 19.
Counsell, Revd Michael, 97, 109.

Davis, Revd Rex, 100.
Dehaquani-Tafti, Bishop, 2.
Djilas, Milovan, 111.
Dubcek, Alexander, 59, 97.

Engstrom, Prof Olle, 57.

Fard, Master W. D., 34.
Feuerbach, Ludwig, 133.
Fletcher, William C., 58, 102.
Freire, Paulo, 27f.

Genders, Bishop Anselm, 22, 23.
Greet, Revd Kenneth, 24, 106.
Greig, Ian, 35.

Hathaway, Revd David, 80.
Headlam, Dr, 128.
Holloway, Revd Richard, 67.
Howe, Darcus, 40.
Howell, Bishop Kenneth, 121.
Hromadka, Joseph, 102.
Huddleston, Bishop Trevor, 12, 106.
Hudson, Darril, 166.

Jackson, Revd Graeme, 98.
John, Gus, 47.
John Paul I, Pope, 72.
Johnson, Revd Dr Hewlett, 98.
Juvenaly, Metropolitan, 67.

Kapuuo, Clemens, 147.
Kaunda, Kenneth, 12, 139.
Kendall, Revd Elliott, 7, 46.
Kingsnorth, Canon, 125.

Lamont, Bishop, 16.
Levitin, Anatole, 69.
Lewis, Revd Arthur, 9, 163.
Luthuli, Albert, 159.

MacBride, Sean, 151.
MacLeod, Lord, 106.
Malcolm X, 33, 35.
Malsbury, Revd Dwight, 117.
Mandela, Nelson, 155-8.
Mandela, Winnie, 163.
Marx, Karl, 26, 31, 133.

McGovern, George, 37.
Michael X, 35, 36.
Mindszenty, Cardinal, 78, 79.
Moltmann, Juergen, 134.
Morris, Revd Colin, 12.
Morton Revd Harry, 3, 43f.
Mugabe, Robert, 16, 137f.
Muzorewa, Bishop, 137-8.

Nandy, Dipak, 39.
Niemoller, Dr Martin, 106.
Niilus, Leopoldo, 113.
Nikodim, Metropolitan, 53, 58, 71, 86, 102, 103.
Nixon, President, 99, 101, 107.
Nkomo, Joshua, 19, 20, 137-8.
Noah, Professor, 29.
Nujoma, Sam, 144f, 163.

Oestreicher, Revd Paul, 12, 16, 24.
Ogle, Dr George, 116.
Oppenheimer, Harry, 39.
Owen, Dr Anthony David, 15.
Owen, Dr David, 15, 20.

Panov, Valery, 84.
Park, President, 112.
Paul VI, Pope, 1, 106.
Pawley, Bernard, 59.
Payne, Dr Ernest, 62, 67.
Pimen, Patriarch, 71.
Pius XI, Pope, 84.
Potter, Dr Philip, 5, 33, 38, 42, 60, 68, 75, 77, 100, 106, 122, 130.
Pym, Francis, 139.

Ramsey, Dr Michael, 21, 36.
Regelson, Lev, 65f, 81.
Rhymes, Canon Douglas, 23.
Rossell, Dr Jacques, 67.
Russell, Dr David, 44, 81.

Sakharov, Dr Andrei, 62, 75.
Salisbury, Dean of, 19.

Sansbury, Bishop Kenneth, 4, 44.
Sawh, Roy, 36.
Shaw, Allan, 13.
Sheppard, Bishop David, 46, 47.
Shipanga, Andreas, 146.
Sieff, David, 39.
Sithole, Revd, D., 77.
Slovo, Joe, 157, 165.
Smith, Ian, 16, 21, 137-8.
Soloviev, Vladimir, 136.
Solzhenitsyn, Alexander, 3, 10, 54, 63, 71.
Soper, Lord, 106.
Stalin, Joseph, 83, 111.
Swaffer, Hannen, 127.

Tambo, Oliver, 156, 157, 160, 163.
Talantov, Boris, 53, 72.
Taylor, Revd John, 124.
Temple, William, Archbishop of Canterbury, 127.
Thieu, President, 97.
Tolbert, Dr, 80.
Thomas, M. M., 122.
Thompson, Sir Robert, 101.
Trelford, Donald, 138.
Tutu, Archbishop Desmond, 156, 162, 164-5.

Vins, Georgi, 73f.
Visser t'Hooft, 58.
Vorster, John, 137, 166.

Waite, Terry, 147.
Webb, Pauline, 37, 50, 132.
Whitlam, Gough, 105.
Willebrands, Cardinal Jan, 1.
Wilson, Harold, 21, 22.
Wooding, Dan, 118.
Wurmbrand, Richard, 79.

Yakunin, Fr Gleb, 65f, 81.